ESSAYS ON THE VIENNESE CLASSICAL STYLE

Joseph Haydn. Oil painting by Ludwig Guttenbrunn
(Wolfgang von Karajan, Salzburg). A copy is owned
by the heirs of Stefan Zweig in London.

H. C. ROBBINS LANDON

Essays on the Viennese Classical Style

GLUCK, HAYDN, MOZART, BEETHOVEN

The Macmillan Company

The Macmillan Company
866 Third Avenue, New York, N.Y. 10022

Library of Congress Catalog Card Number: 74-119133

Essays on the Viennese Classical Style was first published in
Great Britain in 1970 by Barrie & Rockliff: The Cresset Press,
London

First American Edition 1970
Printed in Great Britain

FOR WALTER LEGGE, GREAT PIONEER

Contents

Illustrations

Acknowledgements

Author and publisher are glad to acknowledge permission to reprint these articles from the original publishers as follows:

The Music Review for "The Jena Symphony"; *HiFi Stereo Review* for "Rococo in Music", "The Viennese Classical Period" and "The Dawn of the Romantic Period"; British Broadcasting Corporation for "An Introduction to Michael Haydn", "Haydn's Piano Sonatas", and "Haydn's Masses"; the Canadian Broadcasting Corporation for "The Decline and Fall of Wolfgang Amadeus Mozart"; Vox Productions GB Ltd. for "Mozart's Requiem and the Viennese Classical Mass"; the Decca Record Company Limited, London for "Haydn's *Creation*". The other articles have not been published in English before. Thanks are due to Macmillan & Co., London, for permission to use Emily Anderson's translations from *The Letters of Mozart and his Family*, London 1966; the quotations in the Gluck article are from *The Collected Correspondence and Papers of Christoph Willibald Gluck*, edited by Hedwig and E. H. Mueller von Asow, translated by Steward Thomson (Barrie and Rockliff, London, 1962). For the illustrations due acknowledgement must be made to Professor Wolfgang von Karajan, the Galerie Liechtenstein, the Österreichische Nationalbibliothek, the Benedictine monastery in Göttweig, Lower Austria, and to Universal Edition for the music examples from Haydn's Piano Sonatas.

Foreword

Some ten years ago, Barrie & Rockliff suggested that I make a collection of my essays to be published in book form; I rather rashly agreed, and then promptly became monumentally sidetracked, among other things with the publication of a complete, critical edition of all Haydn's symphonies. Last year, Mr. L. A. Ullstein of Barrie & Rockliff again suggested putting out a book of my essays and the result is the present collection.

Many of these articles were specifically designed at what is known as the "popular" level, which is to say that most of the facts are not buttressed by footnotes, listing of the sources, etc. Since the whole book, with the exception of the article on the Loutherbourg portrait, has turned out to be of this unscientific kind, I have allowed most of the articles to be reprinted as they stand, with only very minor changes.

Buggiano Castello, July 1968
H. C. R. L.

1. Rococo in Music

The word "Rococo" comes from the French *rocaille* meaning "Grotto". The style began its life in France under the Regency (1715–1723), and first flourished under Louis XV. The sea-shell motif which dominates so much of the ornamentation of the period—even to the so-called "shell" pattern of Georgian silver—has led some scholars to imagine a connection between *rocaille*, Rococo, water, and shell. But whatever the symbolic or psychological background of Rococo, its visual and audible features are among the sanest and most sensible the world has ever known. In furniture, architecture, art, and decoration, Rococo flourished throughout Europe about the middle of the eighteenth century, but it would not be an exaggeration to say that, music included, its heyday might be assigned to the period from 1750 to 1800.

If, for artists, the Baroque was a period of tremendous strength, excited and exciting movement, and large, epic forms, there was also the danger that a certain coldness and impersonality could manifest itself in their buildings, their sculptures, and their paintings. It is very difficult for music to be cold, but if it is, it is generally dull. In Baroque music there was a danger that the fugue, for example, might become a form in which the composer's interest in the mathematical possibilities of various combinations outweighed his joy in sound and his intent to please. In the Rococo style, however, everything was gradually reduced to humane, personal forms. The gigantic curves of Bernini's sculpture in Rome's Piazza Navona became transformed into the delicate lines of porcelain figurines. Southern Germany began to produce such porcelain, of exquisite beauty, in the famous schools at Munich (Nymphenburg, after the name of the famous Rococo castle there) and Dresden (Meissen). Vast, marbled spaces gave way to less lofty ceilings and to delicate gilt decorations. "Broken" colours began to be used for the ceilings and panellings of rooms. The stone grandeur of huge Baroque fireplaces gave way to smaller and more practical ones made of delicately carved coloured marble. In short, decoration became an end in itself; it was part of an intense desire from Naples to St. Petersburg, from Paris to Vienna, to make life more comfortable, less formal, more *gemütlich*. Comfort and cosiness were indeed important factors in the whole spirit of Rococo art.

In the field of music, no one thinks of the Rococo as starting any earlier than about 1750. It is always something of a problem to apply architectural and/or artistic terms to musical forms, and in music the words "Baroque" and "Rococo" may mean later periods than they do if we are referring to sculpture or painting. Nevertheless, there *is* such a thing as Rococo music, although it would be quite wrong (as I shall attempt to show in this as well as in my succeeding chapter on "The Viennese Classical Period") to imagine that *all* the music written between 1750 and 1800 is Rococo.

But it was during this half century that several important musical forms emerged, such as the string quartet and the comic opera; and these same fifty years saw intensive development of such existing forms as the symphony and concerto. Gradually, however, one particular kind of form began to dominate the whole of instrumental music throughout Europe. This was the so-called sonata form; one of the greatest musical ideas ever invented in Western music.

In its strictest sense, the term "sonata form" applies to any one movement which can be structurally analyzed as follows:

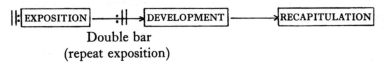

Double bar
(repeat exposition)

This tripartite structure was further broken down into a rather rigid series of rules regarding the sequence of keys the music was to be written in. It worked as follows: in the exposition, the scheme was such that you began with a principal theme, or group of themes, in the tonic (or main) key and then modulated to the dominant (the fifth tone higher), where a new thematic subject, or subjects, was introduced. By the time you had reached the double bar you were firmly in the dominant key. During the development section, you showed your ability to extend, to "develop", the various themes, or parts of themes, and very often to combine them with one another. In order to do this, most good composers had recourse to older contrapuntal forms, so that a simple and singable melody in the exposition might also turn out to be the subject of a fugue in the development section. The recapitulation used basically the same musical material as that found in the exposition, except that the second subject no longer appeared in the dominant but remained in the tonic key.

Although this general scheme looks rather rigid on paper, it in fact gave composers enormous latitude to express their ideas while at the same time preserving the satisfying formal symmetry which had been the purpose of its creation. Just to mention two typical variants, many composers (Haydn for one) liked to preface this entire structure with a slow introduction, a sort of curtain raiser, and it was also possible to add a kind of coda, or tailpiece, at the end of the recapitulation. The form outlined above was intended primarily for opening movements, and the tempo was generally some kind of an *allegro*.

Gradually, the term "sonata form" began to mean not only the first movement, but also to include two or three others. The Italian operatic overture, or *sinfonia*, generally consisted of three movements: an opening *allegro* in the form described above; a slow middle movement in a different kind of form; and a finale in a very quick tempo, such as *presto*. As early as 1740, however, G. M. Monn (1717–1750), an obscure Viennese composer, added a minuet to these three existing movements and created the four-movement symphony that was to be so popular forty to fifty years later.

This may be the place to point out, parenthetically, that Haydn did *not* invent the symphony and he did *not* invent the sonata form—both were flourishing long before he began to compose symphonies. Indeed, Johann Stamitz (1717–1757) composed all his symphonies in Mannheim (South Germany) before Haydn had even written a single symphonic work. On the other hand, scholars now believe that the string quartet in the form known to posterity really *was* the invention of Haydn's. I shall elaborate on these matters in the succeeding chapter, "The Viennese Classical Period".

Opera continued to dominate the musical world in Italy to such an extent that instrumental forms—the sonata, the trio, and the symphony—gradually ceased to exist there as the eighteenth century progressed. In Northern Europe, on the other hand, instrumental music soon became the dominant expressive means of the musical language. In Italy, a new kind of opera had come into being: the so-called *opera buffa*, or comic opera. This stood in sharp contrast to the standard *opera seria*, a popular form used to celebrate marriages and other official events. The plots of these works, generally dealing with Greek or Roman heroes, gradually became merely vehicles to show off the vocal prowess of individual singers. Italian comic opera started life as an *intermezzo* performed between the acts of a grand *opera seria;* it did not deal with the dead heroes of antiquity, but with living persons of that day and age. The new form soon became very popular, and during the eighteenth century the Italians themselves grew further and further away from the *opera seria* and devoted most of their attentions to making the *opera buffa* more complex and more interesting. Yet, the two basic forms of Italian opera continued to exist side-by-side until the very end of the century, and it is interesting to recall that both Mozart and Haydn wrote strict *opere serie* in 1791—Mozart *La Clemenza di Tito* for Prague, and Haydn *L'anima del filosofo* (*Orfeo ed Euridice*) for London. As far as opera was concerned, the Italians still dominated the musical scene in Europe; their composers and singers resided in St. Petersburg and Vienna, in London and Paris. Even Haydn had a large contingent of Italian singers throughout his long stay at Eszterháza Castle.

In Northern Europe, however, the dependence upon Italy and Italian music gradually ceased to exist. The new centre for music in Europe became Paris, which had long led the world in fashion and furniture styles. Music publishing first flourished on a large scale in Paris, long before it was at all important in Italy or even in Vienna. In Vienna, it was still cheaper to hire a copyist to copy out a symphony by hand than to buy the same symphony in printed parts. Parisian taste dominated almost the whole of Europe; the petty German courts made their small copies of Versailles, and furniture makers in Venice and Vienna turned out delicate Louis XVI chairs as soon as the originals appeared in Paris. But although *Musique pour les soupers du Roi* soon became *Tafelmusik* in a small Bohemian castle or North Italian villa, French music as such was less strong in influence than it had been at the time of J. S. Bach. Meanwhile the Germans and Austrians were beginning to shape the fashion of music in Europe for the next hundred years.

In order to show, even if briefly, the function of music at the beginning of the Rococo, let us analyze the various musical forms then in use and their place in everyday life. Opera was, of course, given all over Europe; it was not only given in the semi-private theatres of kings and emperors, but also in public theatres in almost every civilized town in Europe. Opera was, for many of the poorer classes (even in Germany) almost the only contact with music for those who did not play an instrument themselves (which would have been unlikely in a large city unless one had been a professional musician). With the growing ability of the German and Austrian schools, opera in the German language soon became a force to be reckoned with. Haydn's very first opera was a German comedy for the Vienna Opera entitled *Der neue krumme Teufel* (The New Deceitful Devil),[1] and all through the second half of the eighteenth century Viennese audiences could hear both Italian and German operas in about equal proportions.

Dance music remained the other popular musical form enjoyed by all classes. In the famous Vienna Redoutensaal, bakers and servant girls could enjoy Mozart's and Haydn's minuets and German dances just as thoroughly as the Emperor Joseph II and the Austro-Hungarian aristocracy. Nowadays, we tend to overlook what magnificent dance music most of the great composers have left us, and Decca's recording of all of Mozart's dances should go a long way toward showing that while the form was small, the content was large.

The *Tafelmusik* idea soon extended to include all sorts of entertainment, not only music to be listened to from the dining table. In Vienna, street serenades became popular in the middle of the eighteenth century and Mozart composed some of his finest pieces, such as the great Serenade in C minor (K. 388) for wind band, for such an occasion. Another popular Viennese art form that sprang up in those days was called *divertimento* (from the Italian word *divertire*, to amuse). This was a kind of stepchild of the symphony or *sonata*, and mostly consisted of five movements: allegro, minuet, slow movement, minuet, and finale (quick). Viennese composers in the 1750s wrote *divertimenti* for string trio (two violins and cello); for wind band (oboes, bassoons, and horns—later with clarinets as well); for harpsichord with accompaniment (sometimes violin and cello, sometimes two violins and cello); and Haydn seems to have thought up the idea of writing a divertimento for two violins, viola and cello. Out of these rudimentary street serenades were soon to emerge the more sophisticated art forms of piano trio, violin sonata, and of course string quartet. In those days, however, there was not much difference, formally speaking, between a wind-band divertimento and a trio sonata with harpsichord, violin and cello.

In Catholic (and in some Protestant) countries, religious music, accompanied by a full orchestra, still flourished. Like opera and dance

1). *Vide infra*, "The evolution of the Viennese Classical Style".

B

music, the Mass for solo voices, choir and orchestra was performed before every class of society. In the Austro-Hungarian empire, large-scale church music was written by almost every well-known composer up to and including Beethoven. The Mass, for obvious reasons, remained somewhat out of the mainstream of all these other musical developments but it is in the nature of the Church, and thus its music, to be conservative. When W. A. Mozart wrote his father in 1783 to get some of Leopold's church music to perform at Gottfried van Swieten's Sunday concerts, Leopold seems to have written that his church music was now old fashioned and not worth playing, to which Wolfgang replied:

When the weather gets warmer, please make a search in the attic under the roof and send us some of your own church music. You have no reason at all to be ashamed of it. Baron van Swieten and [the Viennese composer] Starzer know as well as you and I that musical taste is constantly changing— and, *what is more*, that this extends even to church music, which ought not to be the case.

Nevertheless, the growth of the symphonic form and the development of the orchestra had a profound effect on the composition of church music, especially in Southern Germany and the Austro-Hungarian empire.

A new factor in musical life was the emergence of the public concert. This was a new idea in many smaller towns, though it was already a tradition in such capitals as London. In these concerts (in Vienna they were called *Academies*), composers gave benefits and introduced their new works to the public, and popular travelling virtuosos performed large-scale concertos. There was now obviously a *need* for orchestral music, and the symphony came to be entirely divorced from the opera and, as the new concert symphony, occupied the attentions of many leading composers. Then the three-movement opera overture gradually shrank to one movement, and the concert symphony came, after considerable experimentation (particularly on Haydn's part), to achieve the form which the older Haydn, Mozart, and young Beethoven adopted: four movements, with a minuet as the third.

Although these public concerts were patronized by the aristocracy, they were also supported by the rising bourgeoisie, who began to cultivate music themselves at home. Central Europe was fortunate in having not only an aristocracy which was musically well trained, but a middle class that soon came to be passionately addicted to chamber music at home. This gradual change of focus from primarily aristocratic and ecclesiastical patronage to a more popular and broadly based support also opened new vistas both for composers and for music publishers. The latter could now—not only in Paris, but also in Vienna—profitably sell Mozart's piano trios and Haydn's quartets to the wealthy bourgeois houses of Vienna or Salzburg or Prague.

Vienna also had a unique claim in that there the popularity of the harpsichord was soon eclipsed by that of the newer fortepiano (German: *Hammerklavier*). So popular was the latter instrument, that today it is practically impossible to find a Viennese harpsichord made in the second half of the eighteenth century. Everybody wanted to play the piano, which had opened up for composers all sorts of tonal combinations and dynamic gradations unknown to the harpsichord—at least in that part of the world. Thus virtuoso organ and harpsichord playing never achieved in Vienna the vogue it had enjoyed in France and Northern Germany.

The overall style of Rococo music is too well known to require elaborate commentary here; but there is sometimes a tendency to identify Rococo with superficiality, which is at best a half-truth. Rococo castles can be splendidly masculine in their way, and so can Rococo music. It is true that composers in this age wrote music in exquisite taste, and that the kind of music that, say, a Viennese merchant generally preferred was a small-scale Haydn piano trio or a Boccherini quartet rather than a large Baroque oratorio. The forms *had* become smaller and more intimate, and the emotions were accordingly scaled down.

In some respects, Johann Christian Bach (1735–1782) might be considered a typical Rococo composer—versatile, cultivated, worldly-wise, he seems to look at us from the famous Gainsborough portrait like any eighteenth-century gentleman of fashion. His music was extremely popular, and in London he dominated the musical scene for years. Yet, there is a side to J. C. Bach that reveals another aspect of Rococo, one that is spiky, uncomfortable, and even slightly sinister: his Symphony in G minor, which has recently been recorded, sounds as unlike Rococo music as anything you could imagine. For in truth, there was a draughty, bleak and unheated backstairs area behind every one of the splendid marble staircases that led from entrance hall to delicately furnished salon. While musicians in fancy livery played Haydn's latest symphonies to Louis XVI as he dined with his courtiers, thousands of peasants in France were starving. There were social and political undercurrents all during these seemingly idyllic and placid years which were to explode with frightening intensity on one summer's day in 1789. On that day Joseph Haydn received at Eszterháza the score of an opera he was preparing for performance at the Eszterháza court opera theatre: *Le nozze di Figaro*, Mozart's great and humane masterpiece, which itself tells us that all was not well with Rococo Europe. It was 14 July 1789, the day the Bastille fell.

Musically speaking, this apparently sudden entrance of the sombre G minor into the placid and urbane world of J. C. Bach is by no means an isolated exception. In the late 1760s, a whole group of *Sturm und Drang* (Storm and Stress) compositions appeared throughout the Austro-Hungarian empire; Haydn was one of their leading producers, but many lesser-known composers (such as Johann Baptist Vanhal and Carlos d'Ordoñez), also contributed furiously intense symphonies and quartets in minor keys, the musical content exploding out of the frame like molten lead poured into a cold vessel. It is only in recent years that scholars have examined in detail the effect of this *Sturm und Drang* school on the history of music, even though they knew that the German literary world had itself undergone a *Sturm und Drang* period, though chronologically slightly later. The title *Sturm und Drang* comes from a play—by the German author Friedrich Maximilian von Klinger (1752–1831)—produced at Weimar in 1776. This was the period of Goethe's famous book *Werther*, and, as with their musical predecessors, the appearance of such works so out of line with previous German literary tradition proved baffling to many people at the time. They should have known better, for art very often reveals the social truths of an age that its citizens cannot or will not see for themselves. In any case, *Sturm und Drang* brought an element of wildly exaggerated, passionate romanticism into an age that had gone to great pains to cultivate moderation and sensibility. It is my opinion that in music, the fusion of the *Sturm und Drang* with the Rococo is directly responsible for the school now generally known as the Viennese Classical Style, the emergence and triumph of which begins where this chapter ends.

(June, 1967)

2. The Viennese Classical Period

We have seen in the previous chapter on Rococo that the emergence of that style was in many respects a revolt against the more severe forms of the earlier Baroque music. We have seen, too, that although Italian music and musicians were still dominant in the field of opera, all through Northern Europe a number of local schools, particularly in the field of instrumental music, had arisen around the middle of the eighteenth century. Paris was now the centre of music in Northern Europe, but other, equally important, schools flourished in London (where J. C. Bach was soon to become the leading composer), Mannheim (where a series of Bohemian musicians were gradually establishing a new orchestral technique), Berlin (which remained rather old-fashioned in its tastes, and where C. P. E. Bach first began to write his major works before moving to Hamburg), and Vienna. As matters turned out, Vienna and the surrounding Austrian empire became the geographical centre for the emergence of a new school which has in the course of time acquired the name "Viennese Classical Style". Let us therefore examine briefly the Viennese and Austrian musical scene about the year 1760.

There were two Court Theatres in Vienna, the Kärntnerthor Theater and the Burgtheater, in both of which plays and Italian opera were given. Various Italian musicians came to Vienna to write operas there, and for our purposes the most important was Antonio Salieri (1750–1825), who started producing operas at Vienna when only twenty years of age. He and his Italian colleagues ruled the operatic world of Vienna and successfully prohibited Haydn from producing an opera commissioned by the Imperial Court Theatre in 1776; and they made the life of Mozart and Da Ponte miserable in the middle of the 1780s. The rivalry between local Austrian artists and the imported Italian opera was not really brought to a successful conclusion until Mozart had demonstrated that an Austrian composer could write far better operas than any Italian then alive. (Haydn also demonstrated this as early as 1768, with his opera *Lo Speziale*, but most of Haydn's operas were produced in the seclusion of Eszterháza Castle in Hungary and never had the effect on the musical world that they would have had, if he had composed them for a public theatre.) Church music in Vienna remained largely conservative, as was proper to the *genre*. Many an Austrian composer started life as a choir boy, and Joseph and his brother Johann Michael Haydn as well as Franz Schubert later were no exceptions. Even today, many great singers at the Vienna State Opera, such as the bass Hans Braun, started their musical life with the Vienna *Sängerknaben* (Boy's Choir). In the middle of the eighteenth century, the leading boy's choir was attached to the cathedral of St. Stephen's, whose chapel master Georg Reutter the Younger was a famous composer of church music and had, among his star pupils, the two young Haydn brothers. Austrian church music of that period combines the new instrumental techniques with old-fashioned fugues in such crucial moments in the Mass as "Cum Sancto Spiritu in gloria Dei Patris, amen", the end of the Gloria; or "Et vitam venturi saeculi, amen", at the end of the Credo. The "Dona nobis pacem" was also very often a fugue or double fugue. Later, the Viennese composer Leopold Hofmann (*c.* 1730–1793) became Cathedral Chapel Master of St. Stephen's, and was well known as a composer not only of symphonies and quartets but also of Masses. Mozart was to have had the job just before he died. Church music was also composed and produced all over the Austrian empire: the great Benedictine monasteries, such as Melk, Kremsmünster, and Göttweig, each had their own boy's choir (connected with a school) and an orchestra, as well as a resident composer, who sometimes became quite famous. Albrechtsberger, the famous teacher and contrapuntalist, began his musical life at Melk Monastery in the late 1750s. At these monasteries, music flourished apart from the church services. From some of the extant manuscripts at Göttweig Abbey, we can see that the monks had music when they ate their meals, in the crypt, in the evening for the abbot and his invited guests; and they played chamber music whenever they could for their own amusement and edification. Some of Haydn's music survives only in copies in one or the other of the great Austrian monasteries.

Prince Archbishops of the Church often had their own choirs and orchestras, too: Salzburg at this period boasted three or four well-known composers, including Leopold Mozart, Wolfgang's father. Another great ecclesiastical centre was Kremsier (today Kroměříž in Czechoslovakia), the resident castle of the *Fürstbischof* of Olmütz— young Wolfgang Mozart played there and the Archives contain some twenty unique copies of Joseph Haydn's music. Still another well-known ecclesiastical centre was Großwardein (now Oradea Mare in Roumania), where Johann Michael Haydn, a composer of potentially even greater talents than his brother, started a brilliant career as *Capell-meister* in 1757, a position that Dittersdorf later had. The principal sup-porters of music in the Austro-Hungarian monarchy were the aris-tocracy, the Esterházys, Trautmannsdorfs, Lobkowitzes, Liechten-steins, etc., who lived in magnificent palaces in Vienna during the winter and in country estates in the summer. All of them had some kind of musical establishment, and many supported an orchestra and a house *Capellmeister;* almost every member of the Austrian aristocracy played some kind of instrument, from the Princess Marie Antoinette to Prince Nicolaus Esterházy, who played an obscure kind of viola da gamba, called the baryton.

Music in the Austro-Hungarian empire was circulated mainly by means of manuscript copies, and with the lack of such things as music critics and newspapers with critics, such as already flourished in Lon-don, works became popular or not on their merits. One monastery copied from another and in Vienna the aristocracy attended each other's concerts and tried to get hold of the latest symphony. The French publishers did a flourishing business with Austrian symphonies as early as the 1760s. (Venier in Paris brought out a whole series with a note on the title page "The names are unknown but they are worth getting to know".) Since there were no copyright laws, many com-posers received no money for these pirated editions and barely knew of their existence.

In 1760, apart from church music and opera, the principal forms flourishing in Vienna were as follows:

(1) The symphony, which had been taken over from the Italian operatic overture and consisted of three movements, fast-slow-fast, to which a minuet and trio were very often added as the third (and some-times second) movement.

(2) The string quartet for two violins, viola and cello, a form which Haydn seems to have invented about 1757. There has been much dis-cussion about the origin of the string quartet, but modern musicology now believes that the quartet as we know it (as opposed to earlier forms,

even using this instrumental combination) was in fact Haydn's peculiar invention. By 1761, other composers in the Austro-Hungarian monarchy were composing quartets, such as Franz Dussek, later a friend of the Mozarts in Prague.

(3) The string trio: this was a popular combination either of two violins and cello or violin, viola and cello. It was the kind of thing one could have at one's country estate without the expense of a whole orchestra.

(4) Piano Concertos, using the harpsichord or the early fortepiano, were very popular, and the leading exponent was the Viennese Court Composer Georg Christoph Wagenseil (1715–1777). The Viennese *bourgeoisie* gradually took over the aristocratic mania for music, and the development of the piano literature in Vienna came about largely because of the enormous support found among the well-to-do upper middle-class citizens.

(5) Piano trios (piano, violin, cello), violin sonatas, and large chamber music with piano (quartets, quintets, etc.) became highly popular as the eighteenth century progressed. The solo keyboard sonata also flourished and almost all composers wrote sonatas for their pupils; many of Haydn's earliest preserved compositions are harpsichord or clavichord sonatas for his fashionable Viennese pupils.

(6) Wind band music. Another very popular genre was the *divertimento* for wind band, which usually consisted of two oboes, two bassoons and two horns. Since the aristocracy had horns for the hunt, it was another inexpensive way to provide *Tafelmusik* by having a wind sextet. This combination, which was soon enlarged to include two clarinets, was very popular for evening serenades. Haydn wrote a whole series of *divertimenti* for wind sextet when he was at the summer estate of Count Morzin at Lukavec (now Czechoslovakia) in 1760; and Mozart wrote several remarkable serenades, of which the B flat (K. 361) is scored for the extraordinary number of thirteen wind instruments; the Serenade in C minor (K. 388) is scored for the more conventional wind octet (with clarinets), but is such a hair-raising piece that one wonders what kind of a serenade the Viennese thought they were hearing.

(7) Divertimenti. Coupled to this wind band *divertimento* was another popular form which consisted of *divertimenti* with two oboes, two horns, two violins, two violas, cello and double-bass, to which one or two bassoons were sometimes added. In Salzburg the serenade tradition, which Mozart inherited, consisted of works that lasted

nearly one hour and were as heavily scored as a big symphony, some-times even with trumpets and kettledrums.

It is fair to say that the general Austrian style of 1760 was *galant*—by which we do not mean superficial; but although the forms in which the works were composed were soon to be used for something quite dif-ferent, as it now stood, instrumental music was intended primarily to please. The form and language were also such that with any kind of inspiration, a composer could and did turn out his works by the dozen. Dittersdorf composed 140 symphonies and Johann Baptist Vanhal (1739–1813) wrote about one hundred; there was nothing unusual about this, as we know from Haydn's 107 symphonies, and Mozart's forty-odd. There was an obvious danger that such music would easily become not only facile but devoid of any deeper spiritual content; for the time being, however, no one seemed to want anything else.

Many of these composers were sensitive and thoughtful artists who must have realized that the great pendulum swing away from the sterner Baroque period had not materially advanced the course of music; and while they might still be in blissful ignorance of the glories of Bach's *Passion according to St. Mathew* and Handel's *Israel in Egypt*, there was enough of their own earlier church music still being pro-duced to remind them that music potentially had more to offer than comfortable street serenades and *gemütliche* symphonies. And so it happened that towards the end of the 1760s a violent eruption took place in all Austrian music. Nowadays musical scholars refer to this period in general by the German term of *Sturm und Drang*, but in fact the great German literary revolution did not take place until some years later, and the play from which the German literary movement took its name, was not written until 1776. This revolution manifested itself in a very curious way. Composers began to re-introduce fugues and contrapuntal patterns into the happy *galant* instrumental forms; it was like pouring ice-water into a warm soup, and for a time you could hear within one quartet a jaunty Viennese minuet followed by a sombre double fugue in the minor key. Almost every good Austrian composer seems to have been afflicted by this passion for counterpoint, and not only Joseph Haydn, as was previously thought. The Spaniard Carlos d'Ordoñez (1734–1786), who occupied an administrative position in the Lower Austrian government, wrote towards the end of the 1760s or the beginning of the 1770s two sets of six fugal quartets which are typical of the trend; so did the Viennese Court Opera composer Florian Leopold Gassmann (1729–1774), and so did Joseph Haydn in a whole variety of instrumental and even religious pieces—the so-called Sun Quartets op. 20 of 1772, the *Stabat Mater* in G minor of 1767, the *Salve Regina* in G minor of 1771, the great C minor piano sonata of 1771, and in a whole series of symphonies.

A great part of this trend also occupied itself with the use of minor keys. In Italian Baroque music, the use of minor keys does not necessarily bring with it anguish and passion—on the contrary. A Vivaldi concerto in D minor is perhaps sober and at the same time restrained, but does not enter into the demoniac D minor world of the Austrian composers of 1770. At the same time, the whole structure of the symphony was broadened. Using the available form, composers infused into the opening movement an element of drama and tension which had hitherto been lacking. They were able to do this because of the way the sonata form movement was constructed. They used key structures to help them in re-constituting the form. The modulation to the dominant for the second subject had long been established, and so had the fact that in the recapitulation the second subject remained in the tonic key. But by linking the whole movement together, and by using contrapuntal forms to increase the tension of the development section, they were able to make the recapitulation, for instance, a highly dramatic moment instead of part of a piece of purely formal symmetry. For one thing, they began to invent strong opening themes; Haydn, especially, was to write them in unison with a striking rhythmic force the motivic essence of which could later be detached and used against itself contrapuntally or even against the second subject. Now all these composers had been trained in formal counterpoint, and as we have said, their own church music continued to be full of these forms; thus it was not difficult for them technically to put all this knowedge to good use. It soon became second nature for them to construct their themes in double counterpoint at the octave so that the top and bottom lines could be reversed. Thus they returned to a far more linear type of composition, whereas their own earlier products were very often based on simple harmonic progressions, *e.g.* the first theme might be a kind of fanfare on a chordal structure.

By 1772, it was clear that the foremost composer in the Austrian empire was Joseph Haydn. Even his most difficult and obscure pieces were circulated from monastery to monastery, and from princely court to princely court. He was the leader of this new revolutionary group, and his *Sturm und Drang* Symphony in D minor (No. 26), even went so far as to weave into its texture a Passion drama of the Middle Ages with a *cantus firmus*, and a Gregorian Chant for Easter Week as the principal melody of the second movement. The melodies were of course known to almost everyone, and particularly to the monks who avidly copied this newest and most revolutionary product of Haydn's genius. Dynamic marks also became more involved; hitherto they had on the whole been limited to *p*, *pp*, *f*, and *ff*, with an occasional *crescendo* in between. Now, we find signs such as *poco forte* (somewhat loud), *mezzo forte* (rather loud), *mezza voce* (inwardly), *calando* (dying away), and so forth. The string quartet stopped being a *divertimento* to amuse and assumed symphonic proportions within the self-restricted instrumental confines. As typical of this whole development, we may point to Haydn's quartet in F minor op. 20, No. 5, which ends with a fantastic *Fuga a due Soggetti* (double fugue) marked *sempre sotto voce* (literally: always in a soft voice, which gives the whole ghostly and definitely sinister overtones); Beethoven used this for one of his models when he was experimenting with contrapuntal forms prior to composing the *Große Fuge*.

Mozart had meanwhile been travelling all over Europe, absorbing Italian music in Italy, Mannheim symphonies in Mannheim, and J. C. Bach in London. Mozart, moreover, returned often to Vienna: he was there first as a child in 1763, and again from 1767 to January 1769, when he had plenty of opportunity to hear the latest products of Viennese composers. Possibly the most important visit was that which took place from July to September 1773, when he had a chance to hear all the latest *Sturm und Drang* works. Always a fantastic assimilator, Mozart went home and wrote six quartets modelled on Op. 20 by Haydn and a Symphony in G minor (K. 183) on which we may for a minute dwell. Among the technical innovations of the *Sturm und Drang* school had been the use of four rather than two horns in symphonies in minor keys. This was done because of the innate limitations of the valveless horn of the period, which can only play the notes of the natural harmonic scale.

Ex. 1

Therefore in a symphony in G minor they used two horns in the tonic G and two in the relative major B flat. This way, between the two sets of horns, they could play most notes of the G minor scale.

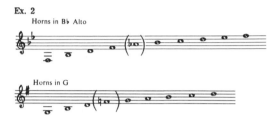

Ex. 2

Horns in B♭ Alto

Horns in G

About 1768, Haydn wrote such a G minor Symphony with four horns and a few years later another excellent one was composed by J. B. Vanhal, a brilliant composer of symphonies and quartets who unfortunately did not live up to his early promise and died insane. To show how quickly Mozart got the message, here is how he was able to use the horns in the finale of his new G minor Symphony.

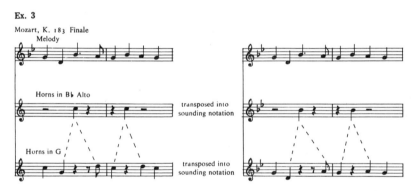

Ex. 3

Mozart, K. 183 Finale

Melody

Horns in B♭ Alto   transposed into
                                         sounding notation

Horns in G   transposed into
                                         sounding notation

For the next years Mozart was several times in Italy and made that long and fateful journey to Paris, where his mother died. In 1780, we find him composing *Idomeneo* in Munich, a work which should have had far more effect on the European musical scene than it actually did (the parallel to Haydn's operas and their lack of effect outside Eszterháza is obvious). He was summoned by his Archbishop Colloredo to Vienna and arrived there on 16 March 1781. He was to remain in Vienna, apart from short trips abroad, for the next ten years until his death on 5 December 1791. Mozart understood what Haydn was trying to do and he wholeheartedly threw himself into the fray. The friendship that sprang up between Mozart and Haydn is one of the most interesting and rewarding in the history of music. The older composer, himself a youthful revolutionary, understood Mozart's innovations, and neither would allow a criticism to be made of the other. When someone protested to Haydn about the beginning of Mozart's "Dissonant" quartet K. 465, Haydn answered, "If Mozart wrote it he knew what he was doing", and when someone dared to criticise Haydn to Mozart, the latter replied, "Listen, if the two of us were boiled down together, we would still not make one Haydn." Mozart's contribution to the Viennese Classical School is in almost every single field; but primarily his great achievements were:

(1) Italian opera. Haydn had long found Italian opera superficial and badly orchestrated, and when he conducted these works at Eszterháza he re-orchestrated many of the arias and very often threw an aria out completely to replace it with one of his own. What Haydn, in his own operas, was trying to do was to marry the new, profound language of instrumental music to the world of Italian comic opera, to create a form in which the audience would laugh but the music would be as complete and as satisfying as a string quartet or symphony. Haydn did this brilliantly in such works as *Le Pescatrici* (1769) and particularly in *L'infedeltà delusa* of 1773, but as we have said these operas were hardly known to anybody except the experts.

Parenthetically, it should be observed that Mozart knew and studied Haydn's operas: a manuscript has just come to light in the University Library at Bonn, which was hitherto thought to be an autograph of Mozart's sketches to unknown vocal compositions, but which turns out to be his variants for an aria from Haydn's opera *Armida* (1784).

Mozart went even further than Haydn in infusing new light into the stereotyped Italian opera; and *Le nozze di Figaro*, the libretto of which was fashioned by that curious and eccentric figure of Lorenzo Da Ponte, turned out not only to be one of the greatest operas of all time but, to revolutionize the form of Italian opera itself. Famous though *Don Giovanni* is, his last Da Ponte opera, *Così fan tutte*, the rehearsals of which Haydn attended with Mozart in 1790, carries to its ultimate conclusion Mozart's attempt to infuse into Italian opera the high standards of the Viennese Classical Style. *Così fan tutte* created just as much scandal as did *Le nozze di Figaro;* it was too much even for the cultivated Viennese to understand, and indeed it has taken 150 years for *Così fan tutte* to be recognized as the supreme music drama that it is.

Having achieved this unlikely marriage in the sphere of Italian opera, Mozart proceeded to do the same thing for German opera. The Emperor Joseph II had in 1778 established what he called a German National Theatre in Vienna for the production of operas in the German language. In Vienna, there had long been a tradition of German opera, but it had been of a very low order, with slapstick and doggerel, though the arias were often of a charming folk-tune character. Haydn had written a famous burlesque of this kind in his youth,[1] called *Der neue krumme Teufel*, which is, alas, lost. He introduced reform into *Das abgebrannte Haus* (*Die Feuersbrunst*), in which the characters are divided into two groups—those who speak pure German (the upperclass) and those who speak in Viennese dialect (which included the archetype *Hanswurst*); the slapstick is beautifully balanced by the ethereal and delicate music given to Colombina. Much of the music that *Hanswurst* sings is of an extraordinary subtlety and is in part very moving indeed. But again, this opera remained so little known outside Eszterháza that only one copy of it has survived: it was recently identified in the Yale Music Library. Mozart's first big German opera was *Die Entführung aus dem Serail*, which he produced in Vienna in 1782. In it, he introduced the new world of the Viennese Classical Style into what is basically a run-of-the-mill textbook. What was particularly extraordinary in *Entführung* was the intricate use of the wind instruments, which created great difficulty when the work was played by inferior orchestras in Germany; and secondly the enormously enlarged scope of the ensembles, something to which Haydn had been devoting his attention in isolated Eszterháza.

Nine years later Mozart produced *Die Zauberflöte*, which Beethoven always particularly admired because he said that in it Mozart had written in every conceivable kind of form. Here the glories of the Viennese Classical Style, with all its contrapuntal virtuosity, manifested itself even in the Overture, which is of a heavily symphonic style such

1).   Recently a document has come to light giving us at least one dated repetition of this opera—on 29 May 1753. *Der krumme Teufel* brought in a relatively high box-office return for this one performance (only four other performances in May brought in more money). See Franz Hadamowsky, "Das Spieljahr 1753/4 des Theaters nächst dem Kärntnerthor und des Theaters nächst der k.k. Burg" in *Jahrbuch der Gesellschaft für Wiener Theaterforschung* XI, 1959, p. 8.

as had never entered the world of *Hanswurst* before. *Die Zauberflöte* has, indeed, everything from the North German Chorale Prelude (with *cantus firmus*) for the two armed giants, to the folk-tune melodies of Papageno, the Masonic music for Sarastro and his priests, to a sublimated coloratura aria for the Queen of the Night, which is a brilliant exercise in how to combine *Sturm und Drang* orchestra with Italian *fioriture*.

(2) The piano concerto. This is a form in which Haydn was not much interested, probably because, unlike Mozart, he was not a great performer on any instrument though he could play any one in the orchestra including the kettledrums. In Mozart's earliest Viennese concertos K. 413, 414, 415, he set the pace for the Viennese Classical concerto; the tone and substance vary from the chamber musical to the grand symphonic style of K. 415 in C, whose magnificence has remained curiously little known, even though Wanda Landowska scored a dazzling triumph when she played it in Carnegie Hall with the New York Philharmonic under Artur Rodzinsky during World War II. As the years and concertos went on, Mozart was to work out an orchestration which, although basically symphonic, was combined with the *pianoforte* in passages that move from the sphere of chamber music to the symphony and back again; in particular his use of the woodwinds together with the solo piano is something unique and a very real contribution to the Viennese Classical Style

(3) Mozart's orchestra. By his use of sinuous inner lines and through his particular affection for the clarinets, Mozart was to create a new kind of orchestral sound. Because of the fact that most of his piano concertos and later symphonies remained unpublished in his lifetime, this rich Mozartian sound did not have the effect on the musical world of its day that it should have had; or perhaps it is better to say that it had a delayed reaction. But by the time musicians in London, Berlin, and Paris became thoroughly familiar with the late Mozartean orchestration, times had changed and Beethoven's symphonies were already becoming known. Thus Mozart did not found the school that he would have founded, had he lived even ten years longer; for after *Zauberflöte*, Mozart again reached the popularity that he enjoyed during the first five years of his life in Vienna. No one has satisfactorily explained the sudden diminution of Mozart's popularity from, say, 1787 to 1790, but as matters turned out it was not his way of orchestration but Haydn's

which was taken over by Beethoven and thus passed on to the nineteenth century. Stylistically, then, Mozart is something of a *cul-de-sac*, mainly because of the non-proliferation of his music during his lifetime. This is not to say that Mozart was a greater orchestrator than Haydn or vice versa, but that their orchestral styles and the details in which their symphonies are worked out were very different one from the other. To the end of his life, Haydn uses the trumpets in something of the *clarino* style which was the legacy that he inherited from the late Baroque world of St. Stephen's church music; and not only are his trumpets high, but he very often uses the horns in C *alto* (high C) with kettledrums which give a brittle brilliance to his orchestra which is very different from Mozart's, where you will never find C *alto* horns in his Viennese period. The trumpets in Mozart are generally used in a lower register and do not dominate; we have spoken of the intricate middle parts of Mozart's orchestra, and this applies particularly to his use of the violas. Beethoven was Haydn's pupil and when he arrived in Vienna in 1792, the Haydn method had become firmly established in all spheres of Viennese music, whether for the church or chamber, or for the concert hall or open air.

People have misjudged Beethoven's relationship to Haydn and Mozart almost as badly as they have assessed Haydn's and Mozart's respective positions in the Viennese Classical Style. Beethoven did not set out to write Haydn's and Mozart's music better than they, because nobody could have written a better *Nozze di Figaro* or *Creation*. It is obvious that when Beethoven wrote his first piano concerto (now known as No. 2 in B flat) and performed it in Vienna in 1795, the second time with Haydn conducting, he availed himself of the musical language current at the time. But even in his first major orchestral work for Vienna, the Dances for the Redoutensaal of 1795, he was not composing either in Haydn's or Mozart's style but writing early Beethoven music with Haydn's orchestra. Beethoven was determined not to turn out music with the rapidity of Haydn and Mozart, and he was very careful which works he allowed to be published. Composing always came hard to him and was the result of constant revision and second thoughts. Beethoven had inherited a fantastic, indeed fearsome, legacy; and he intended to use that legacy for his own purposes.

When Haydn returned from England, he had written twelve symphonies for London which had brought the art of the symphony to a higher plane than had ever been known before except in the last four symphonies of Mozart (which, I repeat, were very little known outside

Vienna, and not very well known even there). Particularly in the second set of "Salomon" Symphonies, Haydn had carried orchestral technique to a new depth and intensity. The drama that Haydn creates during the development of Symphony No. 102 was only paralleled by the development sections of Mozart's "Prague" and G minor Symphonies. Beethoven's first two symphonies were decidedly not rehashings of Haydn's and Mozart's late symphonic essays. They struck off, very slowly, into new territory; but it was not until Beethoven began to draft the "Eroica" that the Viennese Classical Style moved into its great third period—the era of Beethoven. It is not the purpose of this chapter to trace the growth of Beethoven, but to carry the Viennese Classical Style to its logical conclusion, and if we regard Beethoven's later works as belonging more properly to the beginning of the Romantic era, we may perhaps say that the Classical Period closed about 1809, the year Haydn died and the year Beethoven published his Fifth Symphony. The closing years of the eighteenth century in Vienna were illumined by Haydn's six last Masses, huge sublimated symphonies to the glory of God, by the *Creation* (1798), the *Seasons* (1801), and his final quartets Op. 76 (1796–97) and Op. 77 (1799). This golden harvest of the old Haydn is not so much the end of one period as the beginning of another, and this inheritance was to merge imperceptibly with the growth of Ludwig van Beethoven. For many people, the Viennese Classical Style represents the summit of music in Western civilisation, just as for many people Beethoven is practically synonymous with music itself. It was a never-ending period of experimentation and penetration into a new world where the intelligence reigned supreme; apart from J. S. Bach, perhaps never was music so intricate and so dominated by pure human thought. It is no accident that many of us look back upon the Viennese Classical Era with the same nostalgia which the Renaissance man felt for the glories of ancient Greece—when art could flourish and reach an apex of perfection that it has scarcely ever approached since. This is why the use of the word "classical" applies not only to the glories of ancient Greece but to the glories of eighteenth and early nineteenth-century Vienna.

(November 1967)

3. Some Thoughts on Gluck and the Reform of the Opera

A LECTURE GIVEN AT DARTINGTON HALL, AUGUST 1967

A staggering amount of literature in many languages exists on Gluck and his reform of the opera; this literature began primarily as a result of the famous war between Gluck and Piccinni in Paris in the 1770s and has continued, more or less unabated, ever since. It is the purpose of this chapter to re-examine this controversy purely from the standpoint of opera in the eighteenth century and to suggest that in fact the Gluckian reform of the opera might be regarded as one of the most gigantic red herrings in the history of music.

Let us examine briefly the facts of the Gluckian reform. On 17 October 1761, Gluck produced *Don Juan*, a tragic ballet, at the Vienna Court Opera which was received with mixed feelings. No one then or now has, interestingly enough, disputed the beauty of the music; its enormous effect can be judged by the fact that even Boccherini used the music written for Don Juan's downfall almost note for note in the finale of his Symphony in D minor which he entitled *La casa del diavolo*. The next year, on 5 October 1762, the same team of Calzabigi and Gluck produced *Orfeo ed Euridice*, which is generally regarded as the official beginning of the Gluckian operatic reform. Five years later, Gluck produced his second great reformist work *Alceste*, again with a text by Calzabigi. The first performance was at the Vienna Court Opera on 16 December 1767. When Gluck published the score, he dedicated the work to the Grand Duke Leopold of Toscana, later to become the Emperor Leopold II. The foreword sums up Gluck's artistic principles:

"Royal Highness! When I began to write the music for *Alceste*, I resolved to free it from all the abuses which have crept in either through ill-advised vanity on the part of singers or through excessive complaisance on the part of composers, with the result that for some time Italian opera has been disfigured and from being the most splendid and most beautiful of all stage performances has been made the most ridiculous and the most wearisome. I sought to restrict the music to its true purpose of serving to give expression to the poetry and to strengthen the dramatic situations, without interrupting the action or hampering it with unnecessary and superfluous ornamentations. I believed that it should achieve the same effect as lively colours and a well-balanced contrast of light and shade on a very correct and well-disposed painting, so animating the figures without altering their contours. So I have tried to avoid interrupting an actor in the warmth of dialogue with a boring intermezzo or stopping him in the midst of his discourse, merely so that the flexibility of his voice might show to advantage in a long passage, or that the orchestra might give him time to collect his breath for a cadenza. I did not think I should hurry quickly through the second part of an air, which is perhaps the most passionate and most important, in order to have room to repeat the words of the first part regularly four times or to end the aria quite regardless of its meaning, in order to give the singer an opportunity of showing how he can render a passage with so-and-so many variations at will; in short, I have sought to eliminate all these abuses, against which sound common sense and reason have so long protested in vain.

I imagined that the overture should prepare the spectators for the action which is to be presented, and give an indication of its subject; that the instrumental music should vary according to the interest and passion aroused, and that between the aria and the recitative there should not be too great a disparity, lest the flow of the period be spoiled and rendered meaningless, the movement be interrupted inopportunely, or the warmth of the action be dissipated. I believed further that I should devote my greatest effort to seeking to achieve a noble simplicity; and I have avoided parading difficulties at the expense of clarity. I have not placed any value on novelty, if it did not emerge naturally from the situation and the expression; and there is no rule I would not have felt in duty bound to break in order to achieve the desired effect.

These are my principles. Happily all my intentions fitted admirably with the libretto, in which the famous author [Calzabigi], having devised a new plan for the lyrical drama, had replaced florid descriptions, superfluous comparisons, sententious and frigid moralisation with the language of the heart, with strong passion, interesting situations and an ever-varied spectacle. My maxims have been vindicated by success, and the universal approval expressed in such an enlightened city [Vienna] has convinced me that simplicity, truth and lack of affection are the sole principles of beauty in all artistic creations. None the less, in spite of repeated demands by the most respectable persons, that I should decide to publish this opera of mine in print, I have realized how much danger lies in fighting against such widespread and deep-rooted prejudices, and I have found it necessary to avail myself in advance of the powerful protection of Your Royal Highness by imploring the favour of prefixing my opera with His August Name, which so justly carries with it the approval of all enlightened Europe. The great protector of the fine arts, who rules over a nation, who is famed for having freed men from universal oppression and for having set in each of them the finest examples, in a city which has always been the first to break the yoke of vulgar prejudice and pave the way to perfection, can alone undertake the reform of this noble spectacle, in which all the fine arts play such a large part. When this has been accomplished, I shall have the glory of having moved the first stone, and this public testimony of Your Highness's protection, for which I have the honour to declare myself with the most humble respect

Your Royal Highness's
Most humble, most devoted,
most dutiful servant
Christoph Gluck."

Subsequently the arena was moved from Vienna to Paris, where Gluck produced *Iphigénie en Aulide* in April 1774. In August of the same year a new version of *Orfeo* in French was produced at the Opéra and was an immediate and lasting success. There followed a French version of *Alceste* (April 1776) and a new opera *Armide* (September 1777). The next year Gluck wrote *Iphigénie en Tauride* which was first produced at the Paris opera on 18 May 1779.

Meanwhile, in 1776, Paris had requested a new opera from Gluck entitled *Roland*. Unbeknown to Gluck, however, the directors of the opera also requested the well-known Italian composer Nicolà Piccinni, who was then in Rome, to compose the same text. Gluck had the following to say about this situation:

"I have just received your letter of the 15th January, in which, my dear friend, you exhort me to work diligently at the opera *Roland*. This is no longer possible, for as soon as I heard that the Directors, who were not ignorant that I was at work on this opera, had given the same text to Signor

Piccinni, I cast into the flames all I had completed of it. Perhaps it was not worth much, and in that case the public will be greatly obliged to M. Marmontel, who in this way has spared them the misfortune of hearing bad music. Moreover, I do not feel fit to enter into a contest. Signor Piccinni would have too great an advantage over me; since, besides his personal merit, which is undoubtedly great, he would have the advantage of novelty, for Paris has already had from me four operas—whether good or bad matters not; in any case, they exhaust the imagination. Moreover, I have marked out the path for him, and he has only to follow it. I say nothing of his patrons; I am sure that a certain politician of my acquaintance will have three-fourths of Paris to dinner and supper, in order to make proselytes, and that Marmontel, who is so good at stories, will acquaint the whole kingdom with the exclusive merit of Signor Piccinni. I pity M. Hébert sincerely for having fallen into the clutches of such people, one of whom is a blind admirer of Italian music, and the other the author of so-called comic operas; they will make him see the moon at midday.

I am truly put out about it, for M. Hébert is a worthy man, and that is why I do not hesitate to give him my *Armide*, on the conditions, however, which I mentioned to you in my previous letter, and of which the essential points are, that when I come to Paris I must have at least two months in which to train my actors and actresses; that I shall be at liberty to have as many rehearsals as I think necessary; that no part shall be doubled; and that another opera shall be in readiness in case any actor or actress shall fall sick. These are my conditions, without which I will keep *Armide* for my own pleasure. I have written the music for it in such a way that it will not grow old quickly.

You say in your letter, my friend, that none of my works will ever compare with *Alceste*. I cannot agree with this prophecy. *Alceste* is a perfect tragedy, and I do not think it often fails of its full perfection. But you cannot imagine how many shades and manners music is capable of, and what varied paths it can follow. *Armide* is so different from *Alceste*, that one would hardly believe they were by the same composer; and I have put into it what little power remained to me after *Alceste*. I have striven to be, in *Armide*, more painter and poet than musician; of that, however, you will be able to judge yourself when you hear the opera. With it I expect to close my career as an artist. The public, indeed, will take as long to understand *Armide* as they did to understand *Alceste*. There is a kind of refinement in the former that is not in the latter; for I have managed to make the different personages express themselves in such a way that you will be able to tell at once whether *Armide* or another is singing. I must end, or you might think me either a charlatan or a lunatic. Nothing sits so badly on a man as praise of himself; it only suited the great Corneille. When I or Marmontel blow our own trumpets, people laugh in our faces. For the rest, you are right in saying that the French composers are too greatly neglected; for I am very much in error if Gossec and Philidor, who understand the style of the French opera so well, could not serve the public better than the best of Italian composers, if people were not too enthusiastic over whatever is new. You say further, dear friend, that *Orfeo* loses in comparison with *Alceste*. But, good heavens! how is it possible to compare two works that have nothing in common? The one can please as well as the other; but put *Alceste* on the stage with your worst players and *Orfeo* with your best, and you will see that *Orfeo* will bear away the prize; the best things become insupportable in a bad performance. Between two works of a different nature there can be no comparison. If, for example, Piccinni and I had both composed a *Roland*, then people would have been able to judge which was the better; different libretti must necessarily produce different compositions, each of which might be the most beautiful of its kind; in any other case—*omnis comparatio claudicat*. Indeed I must almost tremble at the idea of a comparison between *Armide* and *Alceste*— two poems so diverse, of which one moves to tears and the other stimulates exquisite sensations. If such comparisons are made, I do not know what to do, except to pray God to give the worthy city of Paris its sound common sense again.

Adieu, my dear friend, I embrace you, etc., etc.''

Hitherto Gluck's reform had been conducted by way of the actual music, if we except the foreword he had written to *Alceste* in 1767 or 1768. But from the moment that Piccinni entered the scene in Paris, the reform became a social and literary topic of discussion and all sorts of non-musicians entered the fray. In order to provide a slight background to the actual Gluck-Piccinni war, we may include some extracts from the various letters which appeared in the *Mercure de France* or the *Journal de Politique et de Littérature*. Jean François de Laharpe, a Parisian poet and critic, wrote an open letter to the *Journal de Politique et de Littérature* which appeared on 5 October 1777. Some extracts will show the general tenure:

"On Tuesday the 23rd M. Gluck's *Armide* appeared for the first time. At the moment of writing this article, one can only take account of the effect of this first performance. It was very mediocre. The first act and part of the fifth were applauded. The three others were given a very cold reception.

Such is the general impression. . . . . In the rôle of Armide, apart from the duet of which I have just spoken, this passage roused applause:

Le perfide Renaud me fuit;
Tout perfide qu'il est, mon lâche coeur le suit.

There we have one of those cries of grief which are amongst M. Gluck's great media and which, well placed and well treated, give to the recitative a wealth of expression which it did not possess before him. But when these cries are repeated too often, when one hears them constantly as in *Iphigénie* and in *Alceste;* when even in the arias they take the place of those vocal passages which are both moving and melodious, which penetrate the soul without frightening the ear, and which one so admires in the fine arias of the Italians and their pupils; then one is deafened rather than moved; this harsh disturbance of the organs interferes with the emotion of the soul; one observes that the author has too often put all his expression into the noise and all the means at his disposal into the cries. This affectation to counterfeit nature is very different from an art based upon an embellished imitation, which must please by its resemblance. I do not wish to hear the cry of a man in pain. I expect from the musician as an artist that he will find accents of grief without making them unpleasant; I wish him to flatter my ear while penetrating my heart; I wish the charm of the melody to mingle with the emotion I feel. I wish to carry away in my memory his harmonious lamentation, which should still resound long after in my ears, arousing in me the desire to hear it again and to repeat it myself. But if I have merely heard cries of despair and convulsive moans, I may find it very true to life, but so true that I will not return to it.

The part of Armide, almost from one end to the other, is one monotonous and fatiguing shriek. . . ." ". . . M. Gluck is undoubtedly a man of genius, since he has written *Orphée* and several pieces in his other operas which are worthy of his *Orphée*. His operas are the first to be constructed on a pattern which is both musical and dramatic, whether he himself designed this pattern, as his supporters claim in his honour, of whether he followed that of Calzabigi in *Orphée* and that of Count Algaroti in *Iphigénie*. However that may be, these operas were the first to be purged of the defects found in the Italian and French operas. The dramas of Metastasio, very pleasant to read, like those of Quinault, always presented on the stage a double or triple intrigue, which destroyed unity and so destroyed interest. Almost all his arias were placed at the end of scenes in order to preserve the custom whereby the singer or virtuoso emerged from the theatre after having sung her or his brilliant *hors d'oeuvre* in which the musician employed all his artistry in order to show an actress's vocal chords to the best advantage. And yet this same *hors d'oeuvre* was, and even still is, the only thing that sustains the Italian opera, because little interest is aroused by a drama divided into two or three episodes, besides which the excessive length of the spectacle and the naked simplicity of an insipid recitative also do not attract much attention.

On the other hand, French opera, with its surfeit of ballets, usually divorced from the action, and with its lack of arias was little more than an eternal recitative; one found harmony only in a few choruses by Rameau and melody in his dance airs, the most perfect ever composed.

Orphée, devoid of all these faults, could not but succeed in Italy and in France; in Italy because, apart from its beautiful music, one found for the first time a coherent whole, a spectacle confined within the limits of a reasonable duration, a drama holding the interest by its unity, despite faults of verisimilitude, and finally a recitative which was better contrived, stronger and better adapted to the scene; in France, because one heard for the first time in our lyrical theatre those expressive airs applied to dramatic situations, because for the first time in this opera and in *Iphigénie* before it, formal song formed part of the scene, which previously was dominated either by the soporific uniformity of recitatives or the din of choruses.

Such is the welcome revolution of which M. Gluck is the author and for which he deserves everlasting honour. But by a strange quirk of Fate and by a kind of contradiction between what he did in the beginning and what he is doing today, he may be retarding the progress of an art which he had at first stimulated. Let me explain myself. It may be that the very nature of his talent impels him to flights of harmony rather than to the invention of song and that, being strong and fertile in the instrumental part, he is weak and poor in melody, which, however, like style in poetry, is the happiest and rarest quality in music; it may be that certain specific ideas have become allied to his natural talent; it may be that he had the ambition to create a theatrical music all his own and so to avoid any comparison; it may be that all these causes were joined together; however that may be, it is certain that, with the exception of *Orphée*, M. Gluck in his other compositions seems to have set out to banish the song from lyrical drama, and he appears to be convinced, as his supporters constantly assert, that the song is contrary to the nature of dialogue, to the development of the scenes, and to the action as a whole.

Such a religion could not prosper in Italy; people there love music too much. Moreover, he has only risked his *Orphée* there, an opera which contains music. But in France, where he made his debut with *Iphigénie*, which was highly successful, he may have thought that he would find it so much easier to establish his system, as those Frenchmen who had seen the Italian opera had been mainly impressed by its defects. M. Gluck could find great advantages in building on a completely new pattern. Although there are some fine songs in *Orphée*, those of Galuppi, of Jomelli, of Sacchini and of Piccinni, those admirable airs which are sung from one end of Europe to the other, those masterpieces of emotion and melody in which the composers carry the expression of feeling to its highest pitch and so eschew the false ornaments with which the Italians have so justly been reproached, these great works might offer a comparison in which all the superiority would not have been on the side of the author of *Orphée*. But if the song is removed, if the opera relies upon a livelier recitative, on better constructed and more picturesque choruses with pieces of obbligato recitative to bring out the skill of the accompaniments, it is clear that M. Gluck has created a new art, that he stands alone in his sphere and that his place is unique.

The course he has followed in successive compositions makes these ideas very probable. There is little song in *Iphigénie*; the airs are weak and poor. There is still less in *Alceste*. Finally, he decided to work on an old opera, cut into five acts, full of long monologues, in which there is not a single air suitable for a formal song, if it is not in the ballets; and when all musicians are agreed in thinking that Quinault's operas, though full of beauty, are planned in a manner that is not very favourable to music, M. Gluck alone is unaware of this difficulty. What is one to conclude from this strange enterprise except that the author is persuaded that airs full of expression, which alone are suited to dramatic songs, are not at all necessary for lyrical drama and that with choral recitative, with harmony, one is certain to arrive at a perfect spectacle?"

To this Gluck replied as follows:

"It is impossible, sir, for me to do anything but agree with the intelligent observations on my opera that appear in the number of your journal for the fifth of this month; I find in it nothing, absolutely nothing, to contravene.

I have been simple enough to believe, till now, that music, like the other arts, embraces the whole sphere of the passions, and that it cannot please less when it expresses the troubles of a madman and the cry of grief, than when it paints the sights of love.

Il n'est point de serpent ni de monstre odieux,
Qui, par l'art imité, ne puisse plaire aux yeux.

I have thought that this rule should hold in music equally as in poetry. I have persuaded myself that song, when it thoroughly takes the colour of the feeling it is to express, should be as various and as many-sided as feeling itself; *in fine*, that the voices, the instruments, the tones, even the pauses, should strive after one end—expression—and the agreement between the words and the song should be such that neither the poem should seem to be made for the music nor the music for the poem.

However, this was not my only error; I thought I had noticed that the French language was less rhythmical than the Italian, and that it had not the same definition in the syllables; I was astonished at the difference between the singers of the two nations, as I found the voices of the one soft and pliable, those of the other stronger and more suited for the drama; and so I had decided that Italian melody could not link itself with French words. Then, when I came to examine the scores of their old operas, I found that in spite of the trills, runs, and other inappropriate devices with which they were overladen, there were yet so many genuine beauties in them that I was prompted to believe that the French had within themselves all that was required to do good work.

These were my ideas before I had read your observations. Now, however, you have lightened my darkness; I am wholly astonished that in a few hours you have made more observations on my art than I myself in a practical experience of forty years. You prove to me that it is sufficient to be a well-read man, in order to speak on everything. Now I am convinced that the Italian is the most excellent, the true music; that the melody, if it is to please, must be regular and periodic, and that even in a moment of confusion, where we have to do with the vocal utterances of several persons swayed by varying passions, the composer must still maintain this regularity of melody.

I agree with you that of all my compositions *Orfeo* alone is supportable; and I sincerely beg the forgiveness of the gods of taste for having deafened the hearers of my other operas; the number of their representations and the applause the public has been good enough to bestow on them do not prevent my seeing how pitiable they are. I am so convinced of it that I wish to re-write them; and as I see that you are passionate for tender music, I will put in the mouth of the furious Achilles a song so tender and so sweet, that all the spectators will be moved to tears.

As for *Armide*, I will be very careful to leave the poem as it is; for, as you very perspicaciously observe, 'the operas of Quinault, although full of beauties, are yet not well adapted for music; they are fine poems but bad operas'. So that if they are written to bad poems, which, according to your view, will make fine operas, I beg you to introduce me to a poet who will put *Armide* in order, and give two airs to each scene. We will between us settle the quantity and measure of the verse, and when the syllables are complete I will take the rest on my own shoulders. I, for my part, will go over the music again, and conscientiously strike out, according to reason, all the loud instruments, especially the kettle-drums and trumpets; I will take care that nothing shall be heard in my orchestra but oboes, flutes, French horns, and muted violins. And there will be no more question whence the text of the airs was taken; this can no longer matter, since we have already taken up our position.

Then will the part of Armide no longer be a monotonous and fatiguing shriek; she will no longer be a Medea, a sorceress, but an enchantress; I will make her, when in despair, sing an aria so regular, so periodic, and at the same time so tender, that the *petite maîtresse* most afflicted with the vapours will be able to listen to it without the least damage to her nerves.

If some wicked person should say to me, 'Sir, be careful that Armide mad does not express herself like Armide amorous,' I will reply: 'Sir, I do not wish to frighten the ear of M. de La Harpe; I do not wish to contravene nature; I wish to embellish it; instead of making Armide cry out, I want her to enchant you.' If he insists, and shows me that Sophocles, in the finest of his tragedies, dared to show to the Athenians Oedipus with his bloody eyes, and that the recitative or the kind of *arioso* by which the eloquent plaints of the unfortunate King were rendered must have expressed the deepest sorrow, I will retort that M. de La Harpe does not wish to hear the cry of a man in suffering. Have I not well grasped, sir, the meaning of the doctrine laid down in your observations? I have done some of my friends the pleasure of letting them read your remarks.

'We must be grateful,' said one of them as he handed them back to me; 'M. de La Harpe has given you excellent advice; it is his confession of faith in music; do thou likewise. Get all his works in poetry and literature, and search out in them everything that pleases you through your friendship for him. Many people maintain that criticism does nothing more than upset the artist; and to prove it, they say, the poets have at no time had more judges than now, and yet were never more mediocre than at present. But get the journalists here together in council, and if you ask them, they will tell you that nothing is so useful to the State as a journal. One might object to you, that, as a musician, you had no right to speak about poetry; but is it not equally astounding to see a poet, a man of letters, who wants to have despotic opinions on music?'

That is what my friend told me; his reasons seemed to me very well

founded. But, in spite of my regard for you, I feel, Monsieur, after due
reflection, that I cannot possibly become involved, without incurring the
fate of the expositor who, in the presence of Hannibal, gave a long discourse
on the art of war."

The Gluck letter called forth the following reply from a member of
the War Ministry, Antoine Fabre d'Olivet:

"Monsieur, I had not read the remarks of the *Journal de Littérature;* your
letter, inserted in the Paris journal, made me anxious to read them. What
was my surprise to find that I did not see things from the same viewpoint
as you. One might be tempted to believe that the remarks attributed to M.
de la Harpe [sic] are by a musician and that your letter was written by a
journalist. These little sarcastic asides, the knack of evading the question,
all these subtleties seem quite unlike a famous artist. You seek to escape as if
you felt you were wrong: or is it perhaps that musicians are like pretty
women who want to be loved without scrutiny?

Your ideas could not be more apposite: the song and the periodic song
are frequently misplaced. You have done a great service by restoring to its
function of expressing nature an art which even the greatest masters have
sometimes abused; Italy herself pays you this tribute. But have you not
sometimes gone too far in wishing to follow the intemperance of the passions
and the convulsive movement that accompanies them? Reasonable people
will be very much of your opinion: if in sacrificing all else to pure singing one
stifles interest, if absurdity, which is perhaps too common, has substituted
agreeable songs for a powerful situation, if an abandoned lover sings a
rondeau, a romance or merely a brilliant aria, who would not regard such
extravagances as an artistic abuse? But this is not the question. All we are
concerned about is whether an air written purely and formally (despite the
show of ridicule invoked by it) is not susceptible of great expression. I
believe that there are many examples to prove that it can be; you yourself
have produced airs, the beauty and warmth of which cry out to be sung.
All one need know is how to write and how to place them; with regard to
this, you and the greatest *maestros* in Italy have supplied the proof. If today
attempts are made, I know not why, to prove the contrary, is there not some
justification for being scandalized by the comments of those whose enthusiasm, whether feigned or misguided, is so biassed that, if it were a general
affair, it would do injury to the nation? How is it possible, Monsieur, to
argue that passion is constantly unbalanced and without repose? It is well
known that great movements must not be confined by measure, cadence,
etc., and that there must be the recitative obbligato in which you so excel;

but when Nature, tired of effort, reverts to one sole interest, to one feeling which is the amalgam of the crowd of emotions to which one has been subject, it is this one feeling which remains in all its force and to which Nature returns and is reduced despite herself. Do you then believe that an air, which is well measured, has a good motif, is well executed and completed, does not add to the situation, does not add to the dramatic expression the charm of a delightful song? I confine myself to this observation; too many ideas would involve me in other details; but you are in a better position than anyone to follow these principles to their conclusions and to judge whether they harm the theatrical process.

I am neither a poet nor a musician, yet I have ventured to write on subjects which are perhaps beyond my competence. But has an amateur not some right to speak his mind? Does he not pay for that? Without the amateurs, what would become of the arts? It seems to me unjust to pour scorn upon people who write on an art in which they are not professionals. Is it not enough merely to consider if the observations made are reasonable and honest, without busying oneself with other things? Although I might appear in some respects to hold a view opposed to yours, I am, with the greatest respect, etc. Fabre.''

It is no wonder that Gluck could write on 16 November 1777 "I have been so plagued over music and I am so disgusted with it, that at present I would not write a single note for a louis."

Parisien *intelligenzia* was certainly not all on the side of Gluck. Jean François Marmontel, a member of the Academy in Paris, wrote an enormous article in the *Mercure de France* on 15 September 1778, of which two extracts are interesting in that they show that there were people involved in the controversy who were clearly aware of its historical implications:

"The fact that in Italy operas are changed every year and that in France operas which have succeeded are revived on the stage is due, one must realize clearly, to local differences. In Italy there is the luxury of abundance and in Paris the economy of poverty. Operas are changed like jewels, when riches provide the means; theatrical spectacles become worn just as clothes become worn, when one has no others to choose from.

Italy has crowds of composers: new ones are constantly being trained in her schools; either one must discourage them or hear them in succession; and if one allowed those who emerge to languish, the source both of talent and of pleasure would soon dry up. Curiosity combines with this political reason, and a music which is ever new, together with words already known and modified in a thousand ways by the genius of the composers, must have a powerful appeal to sensitive ears. This assault of the talents in one and the same arena constantly stimulates and arouses the spirit of rivalry in the athletes and the interest of the spectators. That is not all.

Delicate ears demand that music should have a perfect analogy with the voice which executes it: as soon as it is transposed, it is altered. The musicians, in composing, adapt the song to the organ for which the song is destined: they take account of its qualities, measure its range, select its finest sounds: all voices of the same kind do not possess the same degree of flexibility or of sensitivity; not all have the same tones, or some are not so full, so pure and so facile. Now, as a result of the rivalry amongst twenty theatres competing for the finest voices, the same voices are never heard in one place two years in succession. That is why, in changing instruments, one likes a change of music, and the change is inexpensive: a fresh cause of inconstancy. That is not yet all.

Every town in Italy has its theatre, but, apart from Naples and Venice, where they are open all the year round, there is opera for only three months; and it is the only public amusement. It runs six days a week; the whole town attends it every day; and when the season is over, the beautiful pieces which have been culled from it are sung at all the concerts; everyone knows them by heart. Would it be surprising if they became satiated?

Yet it is not true that music-lovers become satiated. Despite all the variations of taste in music, they still take a delight in the beautiful pieces from the operas of Leo, Vinci, Pergolesi, Sassonie, Galuppi and Jomelli: they are collected in pastiches, adapted for the piano, and people never grow tired of them.''

''. . . Let us imagine the contrary and suppose that the wellspring of good music were to dry up in Italy one day. Will the entrepreneurs not draw quite naturally upon their stocks and revive the old operas one after the other or incorporate them in pastiches? So the inconstancy of the Italians and the constancy of the French do not derive from their two kinds of music. And can one say in good faith, can one hope to persuade anyone that the French love M. Gluck's music so much that they prefer it to new works which they do not have? Would this not mean that people still crowd to hear it and wish for nothing new which is not by the same author? This is what emerges from the imagined distinction drawn by the anonymous critic between the lasting beauties of M. Gluck's operas and the fragile beauty of Italian music and of the opera *Roland*.

Roland, one of Quinault's weakest operas, was an outstanding success, despite the efforts of the most shameless clique and despite the care taken to denigrate it six months before in the cafés, the newspapers and the gazettes. For two months *Roland* attracted large crowds in spite of the distractions and fatigues of the Carnival, which do so much harm to the stage, and in competition with the fees of the actors, which is even more damaging to the work whose success it impairs. *Roland* is already known by heart by all who sing in Paris; it is a standard piano study for our young people, and in the theatre it was constantly applauded from beginning to end each time it was presented. . . ."

It is clear that these writers in Paris were aware that Italian opera was in difficulty and that opera as an art form was also in some kind of crisis. But because of the fact that they were largely unaware of the operas being written elsewhere in Europe, they perhaps overlooked an important and widespread development which was occurring in Italy and also in Austria. To explain this development we must for a moment return to the origins of comic opera in Italy.

From its beginning as an *intermezzo* between the acts of a large *opera seria*, the Italian *opera buffa* was by the middle of the century a fully established art form. Thus, two distinct kinds of Italian operas existed: comic opera, generally known as *opera buffa*, and serious opera, usually known as *opera seria*. The second category was generally used for festive occasions such as marriages, coronations, and so forth. The subjects of the serious operas were on the whole confined to figures of classical antiquity, to dead gods and heroes. Formally speaking, they consisted of a series of arias with a duet or two and an occasional final chorus. Naturally, these serious operas were sung by the most famous *castrati* and other singers of their time, and a certain rigidity of pattern had been established so that an *opera seria* was not much different whether produced in London, Naples or St. Petersburg. The foolish demands of these famous singers and the aridity of the subjects made the only interesting thing in an *opera seria* the singers' "virtuosity" or the composers' ability to fill their scores with beautiful music. The drama, such as it was, could only be of historical interest or insofar as it is possible for one to identify oneself with a Roman emperor.

Comic opera, on the other hand, generally treated of present-day people and of typical eighteenth century society: there were people from the upper classes and people from the lower, and in a typical *opera buffa*, you will find the same counts, countesses, chamber maids, gardeners, *contadini* and shopkeepers as populated eighteenth century

Europe. The difference between the two forms also extended deeply into the musical structures. In comic opera, the ensemble soon came to occupy a central position; this was because the subjects themselves, with their typical dénouements (two pairs of lovers united and a foolish tutor foiled), lent themselves to such musical forms.

It is quite obvious that the opera that Gluck was trying to reform was the *opera seria*, and it was also clear that once the Gluckian reform had been established, the *opera seria* was doomed. When Mozart set out to write *Idomeneo* for Munich in 1780, the effects of the Gluck-Piccinni war in Paris were obviously still ringing in his ears; and no one would deny a strong Gluckian influence on the music of *Idomeneo*. But after that work, Mozart never wrote an *opera seria* until *La clemenza di Tito*, commissioned by the Prague opera in the year of his death, 1791. Similarily, Haydn stayed well away from *opera seria* and after *Acide e Galatea* of 1762; he only once touched a serious opera before his London trip.

While the Gluckists and Piccinnists were at each other's throats, a quiet reform was in fact taking place. The charge of superficiality might easily have been levelled on the average Italian comic opera plot and on the charming and melodious music which the Italians composed for it; similarily, the orchestration of these Italian comic operas was rather primitive. There were attempts to rectify this situation. Marco Coltellini, a Tuscan poet who was a friend of Gluck's and wrote librettos for Mozart and Haydn, had already produced a highly interesting opera which he called a *burletta*, entitled *L'infedeltà delusa*, before 1773. In this *burletta* there are five people, all Tuscan farmers, and the whole plot takes place in a village near Ripafratta; the only member of the aristocracy who appears is in fact one of the peasants in disguise, and to boot this Marchese is a hideous caricature, a sort of super-sadistic Count Almaviva. *L'infedeltà delusa* was set to music several times, most interestingly by Haydn in 1773.

Opera buffa was in fact about to enjoy its first period of greatness, and basically the way in which composers improved it was at several different levels: First, by the introduction of serious characters into a comic opera plot. One of Cimarosa's librettists called such an opera *semi-seria*, and there were various other attempts to describe the new mixture, such as *eroe comico* or *dramma giocoso*, and so forth. Thus the form of the *opera buffa* was now considerably enlarged emotionally and also made more realistic in the sense that it was closer to everyday life. Secondly, the orchestra gradually became more and more important and considerably larger. Paisiello, writing for St. Petersburg in the 1770s, used the full Mozartean windband including clarinets, while at Eszterháza Haydn's *L'incontro improvviso* of 1775 included flutes, oboes, bassoons, horns, trumpets, kettledrums, and so-called Turkish music (triangle, cymbals and bass drum). Thirdly, the ensemble gradually came to dominate the musical shape of the *opera buffa* to the extent we know it from Mozart's *Le nozze di Figaro* and Haydn's *Orlando Paladino*. By creating an ensemble of this size, composers had to divide it up into a number of separate sections, in various tempos and using various forms. In Haydn's *La vera Costanza* we actually find a very clever use of the rondo form in one of the finales (Act II) to speed up the emotional tension as the drama reaches its apex. Fourthly, the over-all shape of the *opera buffa* became extremely flexible. It ranged from a one-act kind of *intermezzo* (Haydn's *La canterina* or Cimarosa's *Maestro di capella*) to two acts (such as Haydn's *L'infedeltà delusa*) to the usual three acts and even to four (such as Mozart's *Le nozze di Figaro*). It was, after all, in this form that Mozart was able to cast *Don Giovanni*, which he took care to entitle *opera buffa*.

On all this vital development, the Gluckian reform exerted as good as no influence whatsoever. Thus one wonders just exactly what the Gluckian opera reform accomplished. In order to examine this point we must look to the future.

In the early nineteenth century, Italian opera continued to be com-posed and produced at a staggering rate. But of all countries Italy felt the effects of the Gluckian reform the least: the old *opera seria* withered away and died, or became transmuted into the kind of serious opera that we find in Donizetti's *Lucia*. The emphasis shifted away from Greek and Roman heroes but it is curious to note that the serious early nineteenth century Italian operas generally take some faraway place, such as Scotland, for their plots. To hear some of the lesser produc-tions of the 1820's and 1830's coming out of small Italian towns, you would think that Gluck had never existed as far as serious operas were concerned; the Italian comic opera tradition continued unabated through Donizetti's *L'elisir d'amore* of 1829 and was to reach the same kind of climax that *Figaro* achieved in the latter part of the eighteenth century, in Verdi's *Falstaff*.

If the Gluckian reform had only the vaguest influence on nineteenth century opera in Austria and Italy, it did have a profound effect on Berlioz and in turn on Wagner, particularly the young Wagner of the Parisian *Tannhäuser* years; and yet it might be said that the influence,

D

such as it was, was more of a theoretical than a practical nature, that is that it eminated more from the literature surrounding the Gluck-Piccinni war than in the Gluck operas themselves. It has been widely taken for granted that Piccinni lost that war, but if we examine the facts we will note with astonishment that Piccinni's operas were actually enormous successes. His *Didon*, first performed at 1783, remained on the boards at the Grand Opéra till 8 February 1826, when it received its 250th presentation.

In the light of all these facts, is it not legitimate to regard the Gluckian reform as something of a myth?—not that it did not take place and for good reasons, but that it neither reformed opera *as a whole* nor did it affect the really important operatic form of the second part of the eighteenth century, namely the *opera buffa*, whose reform was effected by a number of Italians, by Haydn, but most of all, of course, by Mozart. And from the viewpoint of the mid twentieth century, is there not a case to be put forward for Mozart as being the greatest operatic reformer of the eighteenth century? In any case, it seems ever clearer that whatever its temporary benefits and effects, in the long view of music history the Gluckian operatic reform was what used to be called in Shakespearian drama a "diversion off stage".

4. The "Loutherbourg" Haydn Portrait

One of the four journals Haydn kept during his two London journeys of 1791–95 is in the Library of the Mozarteum in Salzburg; it is the so-called "third" of the four and was written during the second English trip, in 1794 and 1795. It was first published complete in 1909, edited by J. E. Engl,[1] and on page 23 of the Engl edition we read the following entry: "Ich lernte in Canterbury den Famore, mahler keñen." For half a century, this was the standard text, but in connection with the first collected edition of Haydn's letters,[2] the present writer examined the autograph manuscript in Salzburg and established that what Haydn actually wrote was not "I met Famore the painter in Canterbury" but: "Ich lernte lauterburg den Famosen mahler keñen" ("I met Lauterburg the famous painter").[3] For the first time in the Haydn literature, therefore, we now have authentic confirmation that Haydn personally knew the well-known *genre* painter Philipp Jakob Loutherbourg the Younger (also known as Lautherburg, Lautherbourg, etc.), who was born on 31 October 1740 in Strasbourg and died in London on 11 March 1812. Loutherbourg was renowned not only for his oil paintings —many of which now hang in European and British galleries—but also for his engravings. Later, he often made designs for engravings which were then executed by colleagues.

The name Loutherbourg was not entirely unknown to Haydn scholars. In the Appendix "Haydn-Bildnisse" (Haydn Portraits) to volume III of the Pohl-Botstiber Haydn biography,[4] we find the following entry, under "Stiche, Radierungen, Lithographien usw" ("Engravings, Etchings, Lithographs, etc."):

"Appollini. Tableau: Oben Lyra mit abwärtsgehenden Strahlen; darauf

Joseph Haydn. Detail from "The Likenesses from Miniature Cameos by H. de Janvry. P. J. de Loutherbourg del. J. Landseer sc. 1801, London." (Österreichische National-bibliothek, Vienna).

Medaillonporträts von Haydn, Mozart, Rhode, Viotti, Cramer, Pinto, Salomon, Ranzzini [*recte* Rauzzini], Cimador, Mulmandel [*recte* Hulmandel], Clementi, Yaniewitz, Shimmer, Dussek, Steibelt, Mara, Parke, Banti, Krumpholtz, Henfelt [correct?], Viganoni, Cervetto, Dragonetti, Lindley. The Likenesses from Miniature Cameos by H. de Janory [*recte* Janvry]. I [*recte* J] Landseer sculp. J. S. [*recte* P. J.] de Loutherbourg del."

This "tableau", despite the above description in the standard Haydn biography, seemed to have remained completely unknown. Yet, the name Loutherbourg continued, vaguely, to be associated with that of Joseph Haydn. In an interesting article by Joseph Muller entitled "Haydn Portraits", published in 1932,[5] we read:

"1801
Loutherbourg, P. J. de
Unverified drawing.
Landseer, I., sculp., 1801."

On the other hand, no mention of the supposed Haydn portrait by Loutherbourg is found in the excellent Somfai publication on Haydn iconography,[6] though Somfai publishes a portrait of Loutherbourg in connection with Haydn's English sojourn.

Recently the present writer was at the Viennese antiquarian bookseller Ingo Nebehay—who has always been of the greatest assistance—and purchased there the publication *Katalog der Portrait-Sammlung der k. u. k. General-Intendanz der k. k. Hoftheater*, which has become extremely rare. The work appeared in several volumes, of which volume one, "Erste Abtheilung, Gruppe III. Musiker (Tondichter, Tonkünstler, Concertsänger) und Musikschriftsteller", published at Vienna in 1892, concerns us. On page 169 of this publication we find the entry:

"—Buste, mit vielen anderen Musikern auf 1 Blatt ("The Lickeness [sic] from Miniature Cameos by H. de Janvry-Apollini"). Gr.-Fol. J. J. de Lontherburg, [*sic*] del. J. Landseer sc. 1801, London."

It was quite clear that this was a listing of the long-sought Loutherbourg portrait. An enquiry was made and fortunately it transpired that the Portrait Collection of the Austrian National Library—where the entire holdings of the former k. k. Hoftheater-Intendanz were transferred many years ago—still has the sheet in question, preserved as catalogue no. 510. 347.

As will be seen from our reproduction—the first in modern times, and here printed with the kind permission of the Austrian National Library—the description in Pohl-Botstiber is fairly accurate (the mistakes have been corrected in our listing, above, by the use of brackets and *recte*). Apart from the interesting portrait of Haydn which, it will be observed, is rather accurate and lifelike, the sheet is highly significant for the likenesses of Haydn's contemporaries, of which some are extremely rare and several appear to be preserved only in this form.

The engraver was John Landseer, who was also an archeologist; he was born in 1763 or 1769 at Lincoln and died on 29 February 1852 in London, and frequently collaborated with Loutherbourg.[7] The one mystery which we have not succeeded in clearing up is the sentence at the bottom of the sheet which reads, "The Likenesses from Miniature Cameos by H. de Janvry". We could not find the name Janvry in any of the standard reference books on painters, engravers, etc., and it is not obvious, from the evidence (or lack of evidence) now at our disposal, how much of the artistic work must be laid to Loutherbourg and how much to the unknown Janvry.

The Mozart portrait is not, perhaps, as interesting as the Haydn— Mozart had been dead for some years and the artists could only work from secondary sources—in this particular case they probably used the well-known engraving published by Artaria in Vienna in 1789 (engraved by Johann Georg Mansfeld from a source by Leonard Posch)[8] or one of the other Posch derivatives, such as the Breitkopf & Härtel publication of 1798ff., which used a plate (engraved by Klemens Kohl after Posch in 1793) sold to the Leipzig house by Constanze Mozart. Many, indeed most, of the other musicians shown on this plate had visited London at some time in their careers or actually lived there, and thus their portraits are much closer to life than Mozart's. Where we have ample material for comparison—such as in the cases of Haydn or his impresario Johann Peter Salomon (see the famous Dance profile of 1794 or the Hardy engraving of 1792)[9]—it can be demonstrated that the portraits are artistically good and truthful.

(February 1968)

1). *Joseph Haydns handschriftliches Tagebuch aus der Zeit seines zweiten Aufenthaltes in London 1794 und 1795, als Manuskript zur hundertsten Wiederkehr seines Todestages, 31. Mai 1909, in Druck gelegt von Joh. Ev. Engl,* Leipzig 1909.

2). *The Collected Correspondence and London Notebooks of Joseph Haydn,* edited by H. C. Robbins Landon, London 1959. See p. 292.

3). See the first critical publication in the original German in *Joseph Haydn, Gesammelte Briefe und Aufzeichungen unter Benützung der Quellensammlung von H. C. Robbins Landon herausgegeben und erläutert von Denes Bartha,* Budapest 1965, p. 535.

4). *Joseph Haydn. Unter Benützung der von C. F. Pohl hinterlassenen Materialien weitergeführt von Hugo Botstiber. Dritter Band,* Leipzig 1927 See p. 406.

5). *The Musical Quarterly,* vol. XVIII, No. 2 (April 1932), pp. 282ff.

6). *Joseph Haydn. Sein Leben in zeitgenössischen Bildern, gesammelt, erläutert und mit einer Ikonographie der authentischen Haydn-Bildnisse versehen von László Somfai,* Budapest 1966. The Loutherbourg portrait is an engraving of a self-portrait; see p. 154.

7). The information on Loutherbourg and Landseer from the Thieme-Becker (*Allg. Lex. der bild. Künstler*).

8). See *Mozart und seine Welt in zeitgenössischen Bildern, begründet von Maximilian Zenger, vorgelegt von Otto Erich Deutsch,* Kassel *etc.* 1961. See plate 21 on page 20. The Kohl-Posch engraving reproduced as plate 22 on page 20.

9). The Dance Salomon sketch in profile reproduced in *Collected Correspondence* (see footnote 2, *supra*); the Hardy in Deutsch *op. cit.* plate 512 on p. 241.

5. Haydn's Piano Sonatas

FROM A BBC LECTURE, 1961

Haydn wrote about sixty piano sonatas and their composition spans half a century of his creative life, from about 1754 to 1794. When Haydn was writing his first works, Mozart was yet unborn; and the last three sonatas, which he wrote in London in 1794, appeared when Beethoven, as a young man of twenty-four, had just met Haydn and had been his most famous composition pupil for a year.

The fifty years that these keyboard sonatas cover were among the most exciting and productive in the history of music. In Europe, ten thousand symphonies alone were written, and countless operas, concerti, cantatas, divertimenti—in short, music in every form. There were flourishing schools of music in Naples, London, Paris, Mannheim and Berlin; but of all these, none was to become more important historically and more glorious musically than that of Vienna. For in the long run it is the Viennese Classical Style that has shaped our musical thinking ever since; without it, Brahms, Bruckner, Mahler, Richard Strauss and even Schönberg would have composed quite differently.

This great flowering of genius was not a sudden thing, however. When Haydn began composing sonatas in the middle of the 1750s, he found a well-developed if rather impersonal, collective style among Viennese colleagues, such as Leopold Hofmann and Steffan. Haydn began writing in the accepted manner of his contemporaries; he was not the kind of genius who came to music with a fully developed style, the kind of genius that could produce the "Midsummer Night's Dream" Overture at the age of sixteen. In the 1750s, Haydn's writing is almost indistinguishable from that of his contemporaries. To illustrate here are four musical examples.

Ex. 1

Leopold Hofmann: Concerto per il Cembalo c.1760

Ex. 2   Haydn: Concertino per il Cembalo (1760)

Ex. 3   Haydn: Sonata No. 13(6)

See next page for Ex.4

Ex. 4

C.P.E. Bach: Concerto per il Cembalo Concertato

If you did not at once identify the Haydn, do not feel too badly about it, because not even the best music critic could unless he happened to know the pieces. The first example was from a *Concerto per il Cembalo* by Leopold Hofmann, then a popular Austrian composer, and it was written about 1760. The second was by Haydn, from a *Concertino per il Cembalo* also of 1760; the third was also by Haydn, from Sonata No. 13(6),[1] written about the same time; and the final piece was part of a Harpsichord Concerto by Carl Philipp Emanuel Bach.

You will have wondered why I start with a concerto in three of the

1). The numbers refer to the new *Urtext* edition edited by Christa Landon, *Wiener Urtext Ausgabe* of the Universal Edition; the bracketed numbers to the Päsler edition which Hoboken's catalogue uses.

above cases. The answer is that the sonata at this period is a very hybrid affair, vascillating between *divertimento*, concerto and suite. Now the extract from Haydn's Sonata is very like a slow movement from a concerto of the period, as will be seen; in fact it even ends with a six four chord and a fermata, at which point the performer was supposed to play a cadenza.

One must not think that the kind of music you've just heard is more or less strictly Viennese; the C.P.E. Bach extract certainly is not Viennese. In fact there was a certain international unity of style in those days, extending from Rome to Copenhagen and from Madrid to Prague. Of course there were all sorts of local colourings; but music in society was strikingly similar. For instance, here are the beginnings of two sonatas:

Ex. 5

Domenico Alberti VIII Sonate per Cembalo (Walsh 1748) Op. I. Sonata VI.

Ex. 6   Haydn: Sonata No. 10 (1)

continued on next page

First we have the beginning of a sonata by Domenico Alberti, Opus 1, No. 6, published by Walsh of London in 1748; and then the beginning of a very early Haydn, written in Vienna a few years later. You will not have failed to notice the so-called "Alberti bass", the broken triads which he invented (or at any rate made famous) and which Haydn, and later Mozart, often used.

At the same time, you must remember that Alberti's sonata was published while Bach was working on the "Art of Fugue", and Haydn's early sonatas while Handel was still alive. The Baroque era was, however, being swept away by the new Rococo manner, which was born in Italy and spread like wildfire over the Continent and England. Curiously enough, most composers split themselves into two personalities, one of whom had studied and could write Baroque music (especially for the Church) and the other which was "up-to-date" and wrote sonatas, symphonies and concertos in the new style. No one in Vienna during the eighteenth century ever forgot how to write a good fugue, and we shall see again and again composers returning to the older and stricter forms as a source of inspiration.

In the musical examples mentioned so far, it will have struck you that no one composer among them stands out. Yet as one studies Haydn's sonatas, one sees that out of this "general" style Haydn soon forms his own, highly personal language while still using the formulas bequeathed to him by his precursors. The impersonal, collective sentiment of this early, or pre-classical style does not in any way prevent an artist of genius from surpassing mediocre and secondary talents, and obedience to ready-made formulas is by no means an obstacle in the way of the expansion of their creative faculties; on the contrary, Mozart's and Haydn's genius shines through and transfigures the many clichés—formal, melodic and rhythmic—which were everyman's property.

None of the earliest Haydn sonatas shows even a glimmer of the genius to come: if this is all we had of Haydn, he would mean as little to the average listener as does the name of Leopold Hofmann, Haydn's famous and well-loved contemporary, whose sonatas and concerti were, if anything, more popular than Haydn's during the early 1760s. The one thing that you will find even in the earliest works, however, is his impeccable sense of form: everything is beautifully balanced, and is marked by a terseness, the pithiness which is a hallmark of Haydn's mature style. This is clearly heard in the first movement from one of Haydn's earliest sonatas, No. 2(7):

Ex. 7

This same kind of tautness is also found in all Haydn's early wind band divertimenti.[2] And here one ought to mention that most of the early sonatas were entitled either Partita or Divertimento, never Sonata—a word Haydn did not begin to use in this connection for another thirty years or so. Another point is the overall form of these works: there is almost no difference in construction between this little sonata (I shall go on calling them that to avoid confusion) and, say, a divertimento for wind band or a string trio of the same period: an allegro, a minuet or an andante, a quick finale in 3/8 time.

2). Published in a collected edition by Verlag Doblinger, edited by the present writer.

We must now make a slight detour here into the knotty problem of chronology in these sonatas. The numbers by which they are usually identified were given to them by a brilliant German scholar, Karl Päsler, who made the first critical, collected edition of Haydn's sonatas during the First World War. Since then, however, quite a lot of new facts, including a couple of autographs, have come to light which make substantial changes in what was believed to be a definitive list of 52 works. In the first place, Päsler did not include eight lost works of the period about 1765, thinking that they would never be found. As will be seen below, there is hope that these eight works are not irrevocably lost; so this makes 60, not 52. But of Päsler's 52, three have to be removed: two (Nos. 16, 17) are spurious, and one (No. 15) an arrangement, not by Haydn, of a Divertimento in C (Hob. II ,11) for flute, oboe and strings. And to finish the problem of how many works there are, it has been discovered that one sonata (No. 19, No. 57[47]) exists in two completely different versions, of which Päsler knew only one, No. 57[47] in F. Recently, manuscripts of this work in E major with a new final movement and without the opening allegro have come to light, and B.B.C. listeners heard the first performance in modern times of the new movement in the course of the programme from which this chapter is derived. Finally, Päsler omitted several works included in the new *Wiener Urtext Ausgabe*—Nos. 4, 7, 17 and 18—the last two discoveries by Georg Feder—and No. 28. The latest total for Haydn's keyboard works is 62.

To return to the early sonatas, the first six are, as one would think, all in the very brief three-movement case except for No. 1 (8), which has four movements. Sometimes the form is allegro—andante—allegro, sometimes a minuet in the middle, and occasionally a minuet at the end. These works are all pre-1760. In the ensuing years, there is a slight change: the sonatas have more body, are more substantial in actual size as well as in spirit. Sonata No. 9 (4), which was written about 1765, already begins to sound faintly like the Haydn we know:

Ex. 8
(Moderato)

continued on next page

There is less of *divertimento* here, and students of C.P.E. Bach will notice that Haydn has begun to take over the lean, predominantly two-part texture of the German master. Haydn often related how he "devoured" the "Berlin" Bach's sonatas as he sat in his freezing garret in Vienna, playing a wretched clavichord he had saved up for. This brings us to the problem of the instrument for which these works were written. Concerti, and of course all continuo work with orchestras, were generally given to the harpsichord; but Haydn's sonatas, or at any rate most of them, do not sound well on a harpsichord, and it is clear that they were written with a clavichord (and later with a fortepiano) in mind. The big transition from clavichord writing to a real piano style will be seen in connection with Sonata No. 33 (20).

When Haydn was asked what had been the important influence on his sonatas he unhesitatingly answered: C. P. E. Bach. Actually one does not find much of Bach's manner in Haydn's very early sonatas, but by 1765, Haydn's whole sonata technique has begun to change. There is now a real development section, a new sense of tension generated by the organised use of motifs. The development sections of two works, the first Bach's Opus 2, No. 3 and the second Haydn's Sonata No. 30 (19), show how much of the spirit if not the letter of this new *anti-galant* writing comes from C. P. E. Bach.

Ex. 9a

C.P.E. Bach: Op. 2 No. 3

(Allegro)

continued on next page

E

Ex. 9b

continued on next page

There has in fact been a big stylistic break-through, and the turning point is about the year 1765. Unfortunately, our knowledge of Haydn's sonatas during these critical and formative years is greatly hampered by the fact that no less than eight of them are lost. We know about them, and we even know how they begin, from a thematic catalogue Haydn kept; and the beginnings are, for the student of Haydn, most mouth-watering. Here are two, in D minor and E minor, and it should be remembered that these would have been written not for a clavichord but a fortepiano, the direct forerunner of our modern piano:

Ex. 10a
Divertimento per il Cembalo Solo

No. 21

Ex. 10b
Divertimento per Cembalo Solo

No. 25

We had given up all hope of ever finding these works, when to every-one's astonishment a good part of one turned up early in the autumn of 1961 at a Marburg auction. It was the autograph of the end of the first movement and the minuet and trio of a D major sonata which, according to Haydn's catalogue, began:

Ex. 11

Divertimento per il Cembalo Solo

The manuscript was owned by a wealthy Swiss collector, and after having disappeared into the obscurity of another collector's bank vault, it came up for auction again, and is now in the Berlin State Library. The Trio is a particularly powerful and individualistic sort of movement:

Ex. 12

This extract from what was thought one of Haydn's lost sonatas will give a good idea of the stylistic transformation taking place in his keyboard writing in the middle of the 1760s. Everything is firmer, harsher, more sharply etched.

As we pass into the second half of the 1760s, this transformation, even in what were previously light-weight minuet movements, such as the Trio in D minor (above), are noticeable.

In Sonata No. 19 (47), which we mentioned earlier, we have a good example of the radiant, lucid keyboard writing characteristic of Haydn at his first full maturity. E major—the key in which the work ends—was always one of Haydn's favourite keys, and his music in that key has a silvery, happy and slightly detached quality: the culmination of what one might call the Haydnesque E major spirit comes a few years later, in the Sonata No. 46 (31).

Ex. 13 Moderato

In the late 1760s, Haydn's thoughts turned more and more to minor keys, not only in the sonatas but also in quartets and symphonies: this is the outer manifestation of a deep and profound change in his style. It can be demonstrated that in the quartets and symphonies of other Austrian composers, such as Ordoñez and Vanhal, a similar concentration of works in minor keys occurred about this same time; but in

Haydn the change is particularly striking. It is as if he and his contemporaries suddenly rose up in anger at their own earlier Rococo pleasantries; it is war against *Tafelmusik* and *divertimento*. Consider this portion of the development in Sonata No. 32(44)'s opening movement:

Ex. 14

And even more, the wonderful development in Sonata No. 31(46):

Ex. 15

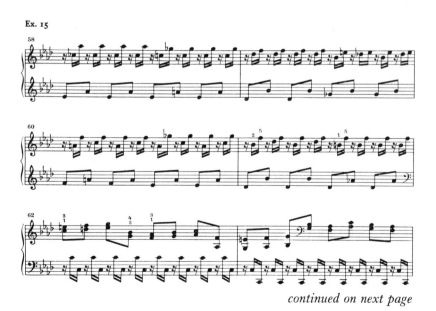

continued on next page

When Haydn and his contemporaries wanted to explore a greater depth of spirit, they automatically turned to the older contrapuntal forms; one now notices how much of Haydn's music is coloured by polyphonic textures. The A flat Sonata, above, comes from about 1768, the period of the F minor Symphony No. 49, known as "La Passione"; altogether, symphonic thought at this time played a most important role in Haydn's sonatas.

The climax of this trend is the great C minor Sonata No. 33(20), written in 1771. (By the way, it is one of the Russian pianist Richter's favourite works, and anyone who has ever heard him play it can never forget the experience.) This C minor Sonata is arguably one of the three or four finest that Haydn ever wrote. In the study of the sonatas up to 1771, what strikes one most strongly is the dark force of the finale, where towards the end there is a real note of anguish and hopelessness:

Ex. 16

continued on next page

especially in the very end:

Ex. 17

The dynamic marks of this work leave no doubt that neither the clavichord nor the harpsichord but the piano is intended: there are crescendos, and especially fortissimos in three places in the first movement. As for pianistic technique, one notices, in the first of the two examples, that the left hand keeps crossing the right—the first time, incidentally, Haydn does this.

In 1773, Haydn wrote six piano sonatas which he dedicated to his Prince, Nicolaus Esterházy, when they were published the next year.

They are just the kind of music Esterházy loved: delicate, highly intellectual (none of that wild C minor stuff for his Serene Highness!), one might say almost fastidious. They are Numbers 36(21) to 41(26). The F major, No. 38(23), is very popular. For one thing, the work has a concluding rondo of the kind that Haydn was to make famous in the next few years—the sure-fire combination of immaculate form, a catchy tune, and ever-present wit.

Three years later, in 1776, Haydn issued another collection of six sonatas, Nos. 42(27) to 47(32). Some of these were composed earlier: No. 42(27) perhaps as early as 1770, the F major No. 44(29) in 1774 (the autograph of this work, by the way, is in a private collection in Basel). The two finest works of this 1776 series are certainly the radiant E major No. 46(31), which we noted earlier, and the ferocious Sonata in B minor No. 47(32). Here is the end of the B minor Sonata, which displays a relentless and a hard, scowling quality that is a long way removed from the divertimento style with which he began.

Ex. 18

Students of Haydn know that for some as yet unexplained reason, the composer had a kind of spiritual lapse in the late 1770s and early 1780s: after the intense productivity of the early 1770s, Haydn had to spend much of his time after 1776 as an operatic *Kapellmeister* for Prince Esterházy. The result was, in non-operatic respects, catastrophic for his creative genius, and about 1780 you begin to have tiresome platitudes like the beginning of Sonata No. 48(35):

Ex. 19

Thousands of young students have cut their pianistic teeth on this wearisome, superficial and boring music (the second movement is particularly empty) and it has given them a warped idea of "Papa" Haydn for the rest of their lives. There are, of course, exceptions such as the fine C sharp minor Sonata No. 49(36); but it is a curious thing that just this bad period of Haydn should have continued to be so popular— the E minor Sonata No. 53(34) is another second-rate work which everybody plays. After a good opening movement, there is a very colourless *Adagio* in which demisemiquaver runs serve to cover up with motion the threadbare pattern and the total lack of inspiration. This is followed by one of those "popular" finales where one wishes dearly that the Alberti bass and the rondo form had never been invented. The best of this group is the famous No. 50(37) in D major, with its rolling Handelian grandeur in the deliberately archaic slow movement. The worst is the first movement of Sonata No. 57 (47) (the rest was composed, as you will remember, many years before): this *Moderato* is in fact so bad that the great Danish Haydn scholar, Professor Jens Peter Larsen, has recently suggested it might be the work of a pupil. But it is Haydn, and there is no way to get round its Czerny-like emptiness. After all, every genius has an off-day, even the greatest ones. But an off-day No. 57's *Moderato* certainly is.

Ex. 20

If Haydn's sonatas were to end at this point, we could rightly speak of a tragic decline and fall. Happily, however, Haydn recovered himself about 1785, and wrote magnificent works such as the Paris Symphonies, the quartets for Johann Tost, and the oratorio *The Seven Words*. In 1789, the year he wrote the Oxford Symphony, there appeared a fine C major Sonata, No. 58(48), with a fantasia-like opening movement followed by one of the most witty and brilliant rondo finales he ever wrote. Notice the increased modernity of the piano writing, with the curiously effective octaves and thirds in the left hand:

Ex. 21

From this to Beethoven's *Rage over a Lost Groschen*, both in technique and in swash-buckling humour, is not very far:

Ex. 22

This is followed by a very well-known work, the E flat Sonata written for Haydn's friend, Maria Anna von Genzinger: No. 59(49) in the chronological list, finished in June 1790. Gradually the full glory of the Viennese Classical Style has reached us, even a strong foretaste of Schubert's romanticism. Haydn wrote to Maria Anna about the slow movement, "I recommend it especially to your attention, for it contains many things which I shall analyse for Your Grace when the times comes; it is rather difficult but full of feeling."

Ex. 23

continued on next page

Haydn wrote only three more piano sonatas Nos. 60/62(50/52), and by almost any count they are, except for the C minor Sonata, his finest works in the form. They were composed in London in 1794 for Theresa Jansen, later the wife[3] of the celebrated engraver Gaetano Bartolozzi; Theresa must have been an excellent pianist, for the works are technically difficult, even by Beethovenian standards. Here we have Haydn at his finest: bold, forceful, brilliant: but a style which also allows for the utmost tenderness as well as the dashing virtuosity which a concert sonata requires: for while Haydn's earlier sonatas were primarily for himself or for pupils, these Theresa Jansen Sonatas are for the concert hall: for the excitement of a cheering audience, for candle-lit Hanover Square Rooms. You feel it all through these works:

3). Haydn was a witness at the marriage ceremony in 1795.

Ex. 24   Haydn: Sonata No. 60 (50), 1st. movt. (*Allegro*)

There are other, equally important features, however. Haydn has begun that series of experiments with key relationships that end with the late piano trios and the string quartets of Opera 76 and 77. The second movement of the E flat Sonata No. 62 (52), probably Haydn's last (the chronology of the last three works is not quite certain), is not in the dominant or subdominant but in E major. For a slow movement of an E flat work to be in E was a very rare and indeed sensational occurrence in those days.

Aldous Huxley once wrote: "Haydn lived to a ripe old age and his right hand never forgot its cunning; but it also failed to learn a new cunning. Peter Pan-like, he continued, as an old man, to write the sort of thing he had written twenty, thirty and forty years before." By now you will have realised the gross inaccuracy of Huxley's statement.

Ex. 25   Haydn: Sonata No. 62 (52), end of slow movt. (*Adagio*)

continued on next page

6. Haydn Masses

"I'm rather proud of my Masses", said Haydn, who was a genuinely modest man. He had every reason to be proud. Unlike the enormous numbers of string quartets, baryton trios, symphonies and piano sonatas, none of which he wrote in quantities of less than sixty, and some of which pass the hundred mark, Haydn only wrote fourteen Masses. They cover almost exactly fifty years of his life, from about 1751 or 1752 to 1802, when he was seventy.

Our survey begins on a damp November evening in the year 1749. The young Joseph Haydn—he is seventeen—has been for some years a member of choir of St. Stephen's Cathedral under Cathedral Chapel Master Georg Reutter. Recently his voice broke, and the authorities have been waiting for a chance to get rid of Joseph, whose pretty soprano voice has become a squeaking tenor. Joseph soon gave them the opportunity—he cut off the pig tail of a fellow chorister and was sentenced to be whipped. "I'd rather be expelled than whipped", said Haydn. "Well," said Reutter, "you shall be both". And so, on that unfriendly November evening, Haydn was whipped and thrown out on the streets of Vienna.

"I almost starved", recalled Haydn of these first months when he was on his own in Vienna. He managed to find a friend who lent him enough money to rent a garret in the Michaelerhaus—the place is still there today, at the edge of the Michaelerplatz—and there he began to eke out an existence, teaching, playing violin in church on Sundays, playing organ and composing. A good deal of Haydn's earliest works have disappeared, probably forever, including his first opera, *Der neue krumme Teufel* which he wrote in the 1750s. But some of the earliest piano, or rather clavichord, sonatas have survived, and two Masses.

We do not know for which institution Haydn wrote these early Masses. He was, among his many odd jobs in those days, the organist of the church of the Barmherzigen Brüder in the suburb of Leopoldstadt; and perhaps the two early Masses were written for a Sunday service at the church. The first of these works is entitled *Missa brevis alla cappella "Rorate coeli desuper"* (Drop down, ye dew, from heavens— Isaiah 45:8), from the fourth Sunday in Advent. It is a so-called *Rorate Mass*, a service sung in German-speaking countries during Advent with a reduced orchestra. As its title implies this is a "short Mass", which in eighteenth-century Austria meant several things: it meant first that the text was telescoped in the "Gloria" and "Credo", that is, you often get each of the four voices singing part of the Mass simultaneously. It is unsatisfactory at best. The entire "Gloria" of the Mass lasts less than two minutes. The Vatican has long since put a stop to this ridiculous habit, but in the 1750s custom was laxer and the churches during Advent were freezing cold. *Missa brevis* often meant using the tiny orchestra of two violins and basso continuo, that is cello, double bass and organ; probably there were three each of first and second violins, and the choir would have three on a part. Haydn himself said, of these early compositions, that he wrote rapidly, but without real knowledge of the art. There are all sorts of primitive technical mistakes in our Mass, such as consecutive fifths; but there is a certain charm about the whole piece; and the "Agnus" with the "Dona nobis pacem" has a touch of real poetry in it.

The other early Mass is another *Missa brevis*, this one in F major with two solo sopranos. Haydn had forgotten about the work entirely by the time he was seventy, and was delighted when someone showed him a copy of the work. "It has a certain youthful charm" he said about it. The *Missa brevis* in F is also scored for two violins and basso continuo. Haydn later added a much bigger orchestra when he rediscovered the work in the 1800s, but the original scoring is certainly more appropriate to the work.

After the composition of these two early Masses, there is a considerable gap. Haydn wrote his first string quartets in 1757, and recently one of his early symphonies (No. 37) has turned up in Czechoslovakia in a copy dated 1758, so that we know he was writing symphonies that early, and not first in 1759 as was previously assumed. In 1759 and 1760, he was in Lukavec Castle in Bohemia writing symphonies and chamber music—most of his wind band music, which we have been

F

discovering recently, dates from that period. In May 1761, he joined the band of Prince Esterházy in Eisenstadt and was to remain in the family's service all his life. When he was first engaged by Esterházy, Haydn's title was Vice *Capellmeister*, while the real *Capellmeister* was the old Gregor Werner, a well-known church music composer in his day. Werner was violently jealous of Haydn and it wasn't till the old man died, foaming at Haydn till he breathed his last, that Haydn could write a Mass. Hardly had Werner been buried in Eisenstadt when Haydn wrote his first large-scale church work for Eisenstadt; it is the *Missa in honorem beatissimae Virginis Mariae* of 1766, known in Austria as the "Big Organ Mass". It is a full-length Mass, that is not a *Missa brevis*, and has a large orchestra including two cors anglais, instruments that Haydn was particularly fond of, bassoons, horns, trumpets, kettle-drums,[1] strings and organ, and the organ part is often *concertante*, so that we may assume Haydn played it himself in the first performance. As is immediately obvious, this E flat major Mass is a far cry from the early "short masses". It has an immense dignity and inner strength, and we find in it that division between four solo voices and the choir which is so much a hallmark of Haydn's later mass style. The orchestra is of course used with Haydn's usual delicate sense, and one notices right at the outset that the composer is working with large contrapuntal lines to which the strictly *concertante* treatment of the organ and the nasal, bitter-sweet sound of the English horns lends a very particular colour.

This was altogether the period when the older contrapuntal forms began to interest Haydn very much. In his instrumental music of the next few years, fugues, double fugues and all sorts of the older forms appear in symphonies and quartets. Yet it is used side by side with the new symphonic development, so that one often has the sense of being in two styles at once. If the polyphonic line dominated the "Kyrie" of the "Big Organ Mass" there is a real hybrid style in the "Et resurrexit"; it is a straight Viennese classical piece till the end, when Haydn shows us that he could write a stirring fugue on the words "Et vitam venturi"; just before the end of the movement the organ suddenly resumes its

1). The trumpets and drums may have been added later; in the fragment of the autograph at the Esterházy Archives in Budapest, they are missing. But most early MSS. include them. As I pass the proofs of this book, news comes that the autograph of the Kyrie—which I had searched for in Roumania in 1960—has come to light in Bucarest.

previous function and interjects a couple of solo phrases.

About two years after the Mass for the Blessed Virgin Mary, Haydn wrote a D minor *Missa Sunt Bona mixta malis* which he entered in his own manuscript catalogue of works known to scholars as the *Entwurf Katalog*, or Draft Catalogue. The beginning is magnificent, a sombre D minor entry which reminds one more of a Requiem than a Mass. In 1829 Vincent Novello purchased part of the autograph of this Mass from Artaria of Vienna and took it back to England, where it immediately disappeared; and not a single copy of the work has thus far materialized. It is a great pity, because 1768 saw some of Haydn's finest and most sombre symphonic pieces, such as the Sinfonia "La Passione".

By 1772, Haydn and his band spent most of the year at the remote Hungarian Castle of Eszterháza or Estoras, as it was often called. Here Prince Nicolaus Esterházy had built a magnificent castle with an opera house and a marionette theatre. It was in this year, 1772, that Haydn issued the Prince a gentle warning, in the form of the "Farewell" Symphony, that he and the musicians would like to return to Vienna. For Prince Nicolaus's name-day, 6 December, Haydn composed his St. Nicholas Mass, the *Missa Sancti Nicolai* in G. It is a pastoral work in many respects, and is scored only for oboes, horns and strings, apart from the usual voices and organ part (not *concertante*). The "Kyrie" is in the extraordinary signature of 6/4, which gives it a soft, lyrical quality in triple time; in Austria, it is often sung on Christmas Eve at the midnight service, and for many generations of Austrian and South German Catholics, Haydn's *Missa Sancti Nicolai* is bound up with crisp snow outside and a church filled with candle-light and dimly-seen incense, with the splendid red and gold of the priest's robes and one's breath seen in the cold but happy church.

The next year, 1773, Haydn seems to have written his largest and one of his most splendid Masses. It is in honour of the patron of music, Saint Cecilia, and Haydn poured out his heart in a gigantic panorama of counterpoint, soli and flashing high trumpets. The occasion for which it was written was the yearly meeting in St. Stephan's Cathedral in Vienna of the so-called Cecilian Brotherhood. It must have been a great moment in Haydn's life to return, triumphant, to the scene of his miserable expulsion some twenty years earlier.

To realize the impact this Mass must have made on the Viennese on 22 November 1773, we need play no more than the "Et Resurrexit," which ends with the most tightly-knit and stirring fugue Haydn ever wrote, to the words "Et vitam venturi"; and it really does seem that Haydn was suddenly gripped with a vast vision of Life Eternal and Everlasting, rather like that moment when Handel said, "I did think I saw the Great God Himself".

This is the period of the great string Quartets from Opus 20, of the "Trauer" and "Farewell" Symphonies, of the C minor piano Sonata. Haydn had developed tiger's claws, and his vision of "Benedictus, qui venit in Nomine Domine" (Blessed is He that walketh in the Name of the Lord), is one of an Old Testament prophet. He was to return to this stern concept in the *Nelson Mass*, years later.

A few years later, about 1775, Haydn wrote his last *Missa brevis*. It is called *Missa brevis Sancti Joannis de Deo*, and St. John of God was the patron saint of an order called the Brothers of Mercy. They had a convent in Eisenstadt and Haydn was friendly not only with them but with the Vienna chapter, who had been his hosts for the first public performance of his *Stabat Mater* some years earlier. The church of the Eisenstadt order is tiny, and the organ loft is just big enough to accommodate a choir and a small orchestra. The organ is still preserved, by the way. *Missa brevis*, anno 1775, meant quite a different sort of work than it had done a quarter of a century before. It is a Mass on a tiny scale, this Mass for St. John of God, but it contains some wonderful things.

Perhaps the finest moment is the "Agnus Dei", with its beautiful "Dona nobis pacem", in which everything dies away to a pianissimo hush. It is miniature art on the finest level.

One of Haydn's friends was a retired military man—Haydn's friends came from all sorts of different professions and included monks, ladies-in-waiting, doctors, dentists, actors, aristocrats, cobblers—everything you can think of. This retired military man who had been in Supplies, was elevated to the nobility by Maria Theresa in March 1781, and Anton Liebe von Kreutzner asked Haydn to write a festive Mass to celebrate the event in the famous pilgrimage church of Mariazell, in Styria. Haydn had made the long pilgrimage from Vienna to Mariazell on foot himself, as a young man, and had been invited to stay with the monks there. We can easily imagine the old Herr von Kreutzner, weary from his long trip on foot, listening, sometime in the Summer of 1782, to the new Mass in the coolness of the huge Baroque church at Mariazell. Haydn called the work *Missa Cellensis*, Celle being Zell in German, and thus the Mass is known in Austria as the *Mariazeller-messe*. By this time, Haydn had conceived the idea of casting some of the movements of the Mass in sonata form. As is well known, Haydn took a rather stand-off-ish view of the second subject and often abolished it entirely; so one is not surprised to find, in the "Kyrie" of his *Maria-zellermesse*, that the second subject, the "Christe eleison", is simply the main tune in the dominant. One also notes how closely he has woven symphonic thought to choral and orchestral texture. There is a magnificent slow introduction, where the voices seem to rise from the depths crying "Kyrie eleison", and then the fast movement. It has the kind of melody that Herr von Kreutzner, or anyone else, would remember; for Haydn was now concerned that his great science of composition should be made popular as well, something that Mozart also successfully attempted with the last series of Masses for Salzburg. Like the *St. Cecilia Mass*, our *Mariazellermesse* has a big orchestra with brilliant parts for the trumpets and kettledrums.

Another wonderful movement is the "Sanctus", with its long pauses. The melody has been discovered to be an old *Marienlied*, or a song to the Virgin, which the pilgrims used to sing on their way to Mariazell.

To end the work Haydn writes one of his large-scale fugues; it makes a powerful conclusion to a work which, rather fantastically, unites Viennese symphonic style, straight fugues, pilgrimage songs, sonata form and even a whole movement, the "Benedictus", lifted from one of Haydn's operas, *Il mondo della luna* (1777), where the aria becomes a lovely quartet for the four soloists. In 1782, the chamber, the great hall, the opera house and the church were much closer than they are today, and who is to say if our strict and puritanical division has made life better.

This was the last Mass that Haydn wrote for many years. As we all know, he went to London twice, and returned rich and famous in the early autumn of 1795. His fourth Prince Esterházy, Nicolaus II, required only of his world-renowned *Capellmeister* that he write a Mass every year for the Name Day of his beautiful Princess, Maria Hermenegild, in September. Nicolaus had no use for the isolation of Eszterháza and lived in the winters in Vienna and summers in Eisenstadt, the castle of which he modernized and improved. There was a new church in Eisenstadt, too, because the Princely chapel was very small and suitable only for intimate family services. This church was called the *Bergkirche*, or Church on the Hill, and in it Haydn conducted his yearly Mass for the Princess, of whom he was very fond.[2]

2). While in London he had dedicated to her three of his finest piano Trios (Op. 71, published by Preston in the Spring of 1795).

The first of these six great Masses was written in 1796, when Napolean's armies were driving towards Austria and actually occupied Graz. The Imperial Capital was nervous and Haydn called his new Mass *Missa in tempore belli* (Mass in Time of War). The kettledrums enter the prayer "Agnus Dei, qui tollis peccata mundi", and provide a sinister undercurrent which then explodes like one of Napoleon's shells into the "Dona nobis pacem".

The second Mass Haydn wrote also dates from 1796, but was not finished or performed until September 1797. It is entitled *Missa Sancti Bernardi de Offida*, in honour of a Portuguese monk, Bernard of Offida, whom the Vatican beatified about this time. It is in B flat, which was to become a favourite key for Haydn's late Masses. Incidentally, Haydn seems to have discovered the unique quality of trumpets and drums in B flat when he was in London; he wrote the Sinfonia Concertante and Symphonies 98 and 102 in that key, and as far as we can determine, hardly anyone before him had ever used trumpets and timpani in B flat.[3] They have a sonorous, un-aggressive, almost shining quality which is entirely different from their sound in C or D major. Haydn now had clarinets as well as the other wind instruments, and he uses them in all except one of these late Masses. In B flat major, too, the voices are nicely spread: the comfortable top for the sopranos is a high B flat, and for the basses a low F means a dominant bottom.

Haydn's *Missa Sancti Bernardi de Offida* is in many ways the most fervent of all his Masses. It has some fantastically involved contrapuntal tricks, including a sort of perpetual canon in the "Et Incarnatus Est". And in the "Gratias" movement, Haydn worked it out so that large sections are in double counterpoint at the octave, that is, put at its most simple, he can turn round the top and bottom lines; he also inverts them and the inversion, too, is in double counterpoint. But these are purely musical means to achieve the rapturous, almost ecstatic content.

Haydn's next work for the Princess is the famous *Missa in Angustiis* (*angustiis* means narrow, straight, shut-in), known as the "Nelson Mass." It was composed when Nelson was fighting the Battle of

3). An exception is a symphony by Haydn's brother Johann Michael written in 1788.

Princess Marie Hermenegild Esterházy, née Liechtenstein. Oil painting by Angelika Kauffmann (Rome,
1795; now in Gallerie Liechtenstein, Vienna).

Abukir, the news of which, when it reached Vienna, caused people to weep openly for joy. They thought Napoleon was finished. Haydn thought so too, though he could not have known of the battle before the Mass had been finished. If you might paraphrase the Latin title, it is a "Mass in Time of Fear". It was the Summer of 1798, and to Haydn, Napoleon must have seemed like the Anti-Christ himself, and Nelson like the Archangel Gabriel. When Nelson arrived in Vienna a couple of years later, he and Haydn took to each other at once. Nelson gave him the watch he wore at Abukir and Haydn gave his quill pen to the British hero. The Mass which bears Nelson's name is in D minor and has no wind instruments at all. It is scored for only three trumpets and kettledrums, apart from the voices, strings and organ. It is the most sombre Haydn Mass on the one hand, but it rises to supreme heights of ecstasy on the other.

In 1799, Haydn wrote what is known as the "Theresa Mass". It got the name for a wrong reason, because people connected it with the Empress Marie Therese—not Maria Theresa—who was the wife of Franz I; anyway it was thought she had something to do with the Mass, which, it turns out, was not true. Marie Therese did have something to do with Haydn, as we shall see later, but it was not with this Mass. It is again in B flat, as are all the remaining Haydn Masses, and is scored for clarinets, trumpets, drums and the usual strings, organ and voices. It has always been a very popular Haydn Mass, but personally I do not think it measures up to the others. It has a sweet and radiant quality about it but I at least feel that it misses some of the grandeur and force of its fellows.

One of Haydn's very greatest works is his penultimate Mass of 1801, again in B flat major, known in Austria as the *Schöpfungsmesse* (*Schöpfung* means Creation), because Haydn used a fragment from his oratorio *The Creation* in it. It is one of the largest of these works, and like the *Missa Sancti Bernardi* it has a fervent quality, an intensity, which begins to assert itself even in the introduction.

By this time—Haydn was sixty-nine—the composer had a fantastic ability to project huge lines. One must remember that after London he never wrote another symphony, and in a certain sense, these late masses are transfigurations of his orchestral works, enormous works which are, you might say, symphonies for God. Haydn was one of music's greatest craftsmen, and he knew of no higher dedication for his craft than to write Masses which, like all his scores, he began "In Nomine Domini" and concluded "Laus Deo".

When Haydn began his last Mass, and indeed his last completed work (excepting some pot-boilers of Scottish songs), he was seventy; it was 1802, and he felt immeasurably weary. He laboured hard on this large and imposing work, which is called *Harmoniemesse*, or Wind Band Mass, because of the use of a large woodwind and brass choir—flutes, oboes, clarinets, bassoons, horns, trumpets, timpani. Much of the music has a particular sense of dignity about it, as if Haydn were aware that this was to be his swan song. The autograph itself, like that of the preceding *Schöpfungsmesse*, is a model of calligraphical neatness. The thin, spidery handwriting, so precise, is now shaky, the pen trembles as he sets his "In Nomine Domini, di me giuseppe Haydn manu propria" on the top of the page.

This has been a survey of Haydn's Masses, but I want to end it with a work which is not, strictly speaking, a Mass, but which sums up in one short burst of fervour and splendour Haydn's late church music. It is the great "Te Deum for the Empress", which Haydn composed for Marie Therese about 1799. In it, he turned to the old Gregorian Te Deum melody, which one discovers in the middle parts of the orchestral introduction and when the voices enter. It is in three short movements, with a magnificent, thoughtful middle *Adagio* which shows how close to *The Creation* it is, and it ends with a double fugue, "In te, Domine, speravi" which certainly has claims to be one of the great moments in late eighteenth-century music. And I think it sums up this stately series of Haydn Masses in a burst of triumph. "Auf meine Messen bin ich etwas stolz" (I'm rather proud of my masses); as we suggested at the beginning of this article, he had every reason to be.

7. An Introduction to Michael Haydn

FROM A BBC LECTURE, 1966

Most sons of famous composers have been treated rather shabbily by posterity, if we except Carl Philipp Emanuel Bach; and many people even today scarcely know that Joseph Haydn had a brother who was a prolific composer highly thought of in his day. Mozart admired his compositions, and Schubert, visiting his grave, said: "The good Haydn! It almost seemed as if his clear, calm spirit were hovering over me. I may be neither calm nor clear, but no man living reveres him more than I. My eyes filled with tears as we came away." And once when Michael Haydn was visiting his brother in Vienna, he saw some of Joseph's canons on the wall and asked leave to copy them. "Get away with your copies", said Joseph, "you can compose much better ones yourself."

The early years of the two brothers were strikingly similar. Johann Michael Haydn was born five years after his brother, on 14 September 1737, at Rohrau in Lower Austria. At eight he joined his brother as chorister of the famous St. Stephen's in Vienna, of which Reutter was chapel master. Michael's voice was rather better than that of his brother, and as Joseph's voice began to change, Michael took most of the principal soprano parts. He also played violin and organ and was soon able to act as deputy organist of St. Stephen's. He studied history, geography and the classics and in some respects he was better educated and had a more scholarly bent than did Joseph. Like his brother, Michael received but little formal musical education from *Capell-meister* Reutter, and studied Fux's famous *Gradus ad Parnassum*, which he copied out entirely in his own hand (his autograph is in the Vienna National Library). Michael always placed originality in composition very highly, and at St. Stephen's he formed a sort of musical society among his fellow choristers to detect plagiarisms in the works they performed and studied. Meanwhile Joseph had been expelled from the choir and was starving in a Viennese garret.

Before he was twenty, in 1757, Michael was writing large-scale contrapuntal Masses using Fux as his model. In this year he received his first appointment, straight from St. Stephen's choir school; it was as *Capellmeister* to Count Firmian, Bishop of Grosswardein. Grosswardein is a small town in what is now Roumania and its present name is Oradea Mare. I went there in 1960—to try to discover the famous music library, but although the pretty Baroque bishop's palace is still standing, its library was dispersed by German troops and subsequently by marauding refugees. In the organ loft of the adjacent cathedral I found a few scraps of music, all that was left of a huge collection in which a great deal of early Michael Haydn, and probably of unknown works of his brother, with whom he remained in friendly contact all his life, has perished for ever. Incidentally, after Michael Haydn left Grosswardein, his place was taken by Carl Ditters, later von Dittersdorf.

In the five years that the young Michael Haydn stayed at Grosswardein, he wrote an enormous amount of music, sacred and secular. He matured early, and at this stage of the two brothers' respective careers, there is no doubt that Michael was the more accomplished composer. Joseph had not yet received an appointment, though he was to do so in 1759, after which his fortunes began to improve. We know of at least six symphonies which Michael wrote for the bishop, as well as Masses, graduales, offertories, salve reginas and other pieces of church music. His reputation was growing rapidly, and in 1759, the famous Benedictine Monastery of Göttweig acquired their first Haydn work— a Mass in C by Michael. Joseph's compositions do not appear at Göttweig until 1762.

At Grosswardein, the bishop's orchestra played the music for the church services, but they also gave chamber and orchestral concerts in the palace. One of the symphonies, in E flat, which he composed for the bishop became so famous that it was even printed in London under Joseph's name[1]. It is easy to imagine the confusion between the two brothers' compositions in faraway places. Of Michael's fifty

1). H. C. Robbins Landon, *The Symphonies of Joseph Haydn*, London 1955, p. 812, No. 75.

symphonies, many were at one time attributed to Joseph, and one is not at all sure that we have straightened out the authorship of all the many concertos attributed to Joseph. Some, such as the second horn concerto[2], may be by his brother. Michael, as we suggested, was an original thinker. One of his most interesting compositions for Grosswardein is a Concerto in C for solo viola, solo organ and string orchestra, a highly original combination, which is possibly unique.[3]

Those who know Joseph Haydn's early concertos, such as those for organ, will realize that Michael's is a better work. It has more harmonic imagination and a longer line, though it lacks—if one speaks of the concerto as a whole—the pithy sense of form that Joseph's music almost always has. We do not know which instrument Michael played at the first performance; he knew how to play both. But we do have evidence of his ability as a violinist, for in December 1760 he composed a violin Concerto in B flat[4] for the bishop which later was attributed to Joseph. Recently the autograph manuscript turned up in Budapest and settled Michael's authorship, for it is signed and dated at Grosswardein. Judging from the violin part, Michael must have been a first-rate violinist, though of course not a great virtuoso.

The Germans have a useful word for this transitional kind of style; they call it *Vorklassik* (pre-classical). The form is, of course, that of the Vivaldi ritornello type; that is, the ritornello, or what an eighteenth-century English publisher would have called "simphony", the orchestral introduction, comes back several times in different keys. It is the father of the rondo form. Michael Haydn's language is an interesting mixture of the Baroque and the Classical. The fact that much of the figuration is firmly based on material from the *ritornello* is not necessarily classical at this early stage; one finds it in the first movement of Bach's E major Concerto for violin.

The difference between a typical Joseph Haydn concerto and one of his brother's is actually extraordinary. Joseph's music is shorter and altogether far more pithy, but also far more primitive. In Michael's

2). See *Haydn Yearbook* IV, 1968, p. 201, Horn Concerto in D VIId No. 4.
3). Autograph in the Staatsbibliothek, Preussischer Kulturbesitz, Berlin (for some years, after World War II, in the Westdeutsche Bibliothek, Marburg/Lahn.).
4). Published by Verlag Doblinger, Vienna-Munich, in a scholarly edition by Paul Angerer.

work we can sense the intellectual, whereas in Joseph's we have far more the easy, natural musician. Formally, too, Joseph's typically simple three part-form is a far cry from the complex *ritornello* structure preferred by Michael.

About 1762, Michael left Grosswardein and travelling through Pressburg (where he probably met his brother, just a year after the latter had been engaged by the Esterházy family) arrived in Salzburg. The tie between Grosswardein and Salzburg came through Michael's first patron, Count Firmian, Bishop of Grosswardein. Firmian's uncle was Prince Archbishop of Salzburg, Sigismund von Schrattenbach, and no doubt Firmian suggested Michael to his mighty uncle; in any case, Michael was firmly engaged there by 1763. Five years later he married a local soprano, Maria Magdalena Lipp, daughter of the cathedral organist. Apart from an occasional trip, Michael Haydn remained in Salzburg all the rest of his life.

At Salzburg Michael wrote in every conceivable kind of form—operas, symphonies, serenades, divertimenti, enormous amounts of church music—several dozen Masses, 114 graduales, 67 offertories—and of course played the organ and violin in concerts and church music. Young Wolfgang Mozart became a firm admirer of his style and we have several Mozart copies of Haydn's works. To show how closely Mozart patterned his early orchestral style on Michael Haydn's one need only examine the Symphony in D major[5] which Haydn wrote in the middle 1770s. The work has a slow introduction and is followed by a quick movement in which particularly the subsidiary tune and its charming continuation could easily be by Mozart.

At Salzburg Michael was often called on to write elaborate serenades rather on the scale of Mozart's for the Haffner family. Occasionally we find most extraordinary movements in these serenades. Mozart-lovers will recall the *concertante* and *rondo* with solo violin that he introduced in the so-called "Posthorn" Serenade K. 320. Michael Haydn also liked to introduce such movements in his large orchestral serenades. We find sections for trombone solo and every sort of instrumental surprise. Two such movements come from a large-scale Serenade in D, of which the manuscript is in the Benedictine Monastery of Lambach in Upper Austria; recently, various performances have called these movements a trumpet concerto, but it is not.

5). Published by Verlag Doblinger, Vienna-Munich, in an edition by the present writer, also in miniature score: Diletto Musicale No. 20.

Michael Haydn's reputation in his lifetime was primarily as a composer of church music, and recently considerable attention has been drawn to his great Requiem Mass in C minor, composed in 1771 for the death of Archbishop Sigismund von Schrattenbach, which has been mentioned elsewhere in this book.[6] The real sensation of Michael's *Requiem* is that it is indisputably the direct model for Mozart's own *Requiem* written twenty years later. The similarities are too profound and too numerous to be accidental.[7]

Michael Haydn grew old in Salzburg. A few years before he died he was offered the post of being Joseph's assistant at Eisenstadt, but after considering this and another, even more enticing, offer—to go to Florence to run the music for the Grand Duke of Tuscany—he decided to remain in Salzburg. He was commissioned to write a Requiem Mass for the Austrian Empress Marie Therese, wife of Francis I of Austria, and he died before completing it, in August 1806. He lies buried in a side chapel of the beautiful monastery church of St. Peter in Salzburg, a few hundred yards from the house where he composed most of his finest music.

6). See the article on Mozart's *Requiem*.
7). Alone the use of the Gregorian "Te decet hymnus" in both works is almost overwhelming evidence.

8. Mozart's Requiem and the Viennese Classical Mass

On October 20 1740, the Austrian Emperor Charles VI died, to be succeeded by his daughter, Maria Theresia. Charles' death was not only of political importance; it marked the end of the great era of Austrian baroque in the arts. From the musical standpoint it signalled the end of a magnificent period; the Emperor had been a cultivated and intelligent patron of the arts and, like so many of the Hapsburgs, intensely musical. After his death, a distinct decline set in: the State-Treasury sharply reduced funds for the grand performances of church music in the Cathedral of St. Stephen in Vienna. No longer did the high masses there offer a spectacle of pomp and grandeur, and the big services with choirs of trumpets and kettledrums were severely limited, mainly to the principal feast-days, such as Easter and Whitsun. The older generation of composers, too, was dying out, literally as well as figuratively. Francesco Conti had died in 1732, Antonio Caldara in 1736, and J. J. Fux survived his Emperor only by a few months; the younger Georg Reutter (Haydn's teacher and Cathedral Chapel-Master at St. Stephen's) had succeeded to his father's post upon the latter's death in 1738.

Even before Charles VI's death, however, newer and more vital musical forces were at work in the Austrian capital. In many ways Vienna's musical taste had been formed by the conservative taste of its ruler, so that the rather severe (if pompous) style of Fux's and the elder Reutter's masses for the Cathedral was somewhat old-fashioned. But on the streets and in the taverns, in the squalid rooms of poor musicians and in aristocratic chambers, something entirely different was taking place. In the year 1740 the Viennese composer, Mathias Georg Monn (1717-1750), had written a symphony with a minuet, the first to be included in a four movement structure. The raw spirit of the street serenades (*Gassaden*, from the German for little street, *Gasse*—later *Gassatio* and then *Cassatio*) was creeping into more serious music. The eternal swing of the pendulum seemed to require a respite from the heavy contrapuntal learning of the older masters: light divertimenti were preferred to the older baroque suite. In the world of the opera, the stylized Italian taste prevailed in the Imperial Court Theatre; but in obscure little theatres, the populace flooded to hear "Hans Wurst" banter in their own Viennese dialect, and, figures such as Felix Kurz-Bernadon kept their audiences by low, bar-room doggerel, to which the sauciest of street tunes were added. (It will be remembered that Haydn's first opera, written about ten years after the death of Charles VI, was a "Hans Wurst" comedy.) Frequently the Imperial Censors prohibited such pieces on political grounds, but they had no official objection to the new kind of music.

Out of this new style grew Haydn's earliest string quartets and divertimenti (which he often entitled 'Cassatio'), and even the contemporary Viennese symphony had much of the atmosphere of the divertimento in its form and melody. The North Germans protested about this "terrible new style," with its hated minuets and its "curious emphasis on the comic." "Recently," writes a North German periodical of 1768, "a Leipzig composer has taken this [Haydn] symphony and removed the excrescencies, to put it into a somewhat more bearable form." The North Germans, however, were like twigs in the path of an avalanche; their composers, even C. P. E. Bach, tried desperately to retain the more severe style; but it was only a matter of a few years before the new Viennese music spread all over Europe, from Madrid to London, and from Stockholm to Paris.

The curious thing about this early Viennese style was its compartmentalization. The average Austrian composer of the mid-eighteenth century wrote in several styles: there was one for these light-hearted divertimenti and symphonies; another for the concerti (which was still very much tied to the baroque); another for Italian operas; and still another for church music. It seems hard to believe, for example, that the young Haydn wrote the quartets of Opera 1 and 2 as well as the Missa brevis in F major; but to him it was quite natural that one should compose string quartets in the new style and church music in the traditional way he had learned from Georg Reutter, Jr. And thus it is that Mozart wrote his early church music in an antiquated style (one thinks of the Missa brevis in D minor, K. 65, with its stiff, traditional polyphony, written a month after the saucy, elegant Symphony in D, K. 48).

This dualistic approach between secular and religious Viennese music continued from 1740 to about 1770, and during these three decades the cleft, if anything, widened even more than before. The Viennese symphony developed gradually in the hands of Haydn, his brother Michael, Dittersdorf, Gassmann, Ordoñez, Hofmann, and a host of others; the string quartet and clavier sonata outgrew their divertimento-like origins and became vehicles more suited to intellectual thoughts. And then, towards the end of the 1760s, another sweeping change began to take place. We can find faint warnings of the change in Haydn's symphonies of the middle 'sixties: an increasingly serious tone, a preoccupation with the development section of the first movements, a tendency to write symphonies in the old church sonata scheme (*i.e.*, with an opening slow movement).

What happened is, however, quite unparalleled in the history of music. Suddenly the whole Viennese school seemed to revolt against its own style, more particularly against the light divertimento-like treatment of the symphony, sonata, and string quartet. Symphony after symphony in the minor key appear in the contemporary catalogues; Haydn, Vanhal, Koželuch, Ordoñez and W. A. Mozart all write *Sturm und Drang* symphonies in G minor within a few years of each other. Haydn's quartets of Opera 17 (1771) and 20 (1772) and Ordoñez quartets of Opera 1 and 2 end with furiously concentrated fugal movements. The adagios and andantes of all Viennese instrumental music become imbued with romantic thoughts; highly expressive dynamic marks begin to appear—*crescendo, forzato, con espressione* (the profusion of dynamic marks found in the Mannheim school never seemed to attract the Viennese much). Haydn writes his great Piano Sonata in C minor (No. 20 in the Päsler list, No. 33 in Universal Edition's); Vanhal writes stormy and emotional symphonies in E minor, D minor, A minor and C minor; Ordoñez, Gassmann and Haydn write string quartets in F minor, G minor, C minor which occasionally reach the depths of passion and despair. In a word, the great period of Viennese classical music has begun. (Hitherto it has been suggested that this period of *Sturm und Drang* began in Haydn; but recent musicological research has shown that it was a reaction which extended throughout the Viennese school; and if Haydn's works of *c.* 1768–1774 perhaps express the new movement at its noblest level, it can be demonstrated that he was by no means alone in attempting to deepen and intellectualize the existing instrumental and vocal forms).

One significant aspect of this *Sturm und Drang* trend deserves special mention: namely, the conscious return to older baroque language. It was found that the light divertimento style and instrumental texture did not allow for emotional expansion, and so the Viennese school drew on their rich contrapuntal heritage, with which they combined the new intellectual symphonic form: the development of motives was thus linked to contrapuntal forms, and we find an increasing preoccupation with fugue-*cum*-sonata, development-*cum*-polyphony, and so forth. Having returned to the baroque for their inspiration, and having combined this with the new principles of sonata form, a new type of music emerged. And by comparison, the church music of the period no longer seemed quite so old-fashioned. The fugue, for instance, was no longer an antiquated mode of expression: on the contrary, it represented the highest level of emotional and musical thought.

It was obvious, therefore, that the contemporary Viennese church music should benefit from this revitalization. Just as contemporary superficiality was banned from instrumental music, so a similar attempt was made to deepen and enrich the music for the church. For many years, Austrian music had been strongly influenced by its Southern neighbour, Italy; the sweet, rather feminine grace of a Pergolesi appealed to Austrians. We find many such Pergolesi-inspired arias, often in a light 3/8 metre, in contemporary Austrian church music; but there is undoubtedly something incongruous about this operatic style when it appears as the "Gratias" of a Mass, and the juxtaposition of this pseudo-operatic aria with stiff, neo-baroque fugues produced a Mass which can hardly be considered the highest level of music (even apart from the question of its fitness for a church service).

That such a composer as Haydn recognized the need for a musical (if not a religious) reform is made clear by his first examples of church music written after the great stylistic revolution of the late 1760s and early 1770s: the Salve Regina in G minor (1771) and the Stabat Mater (1767). In both these works we find not only "new" romantic style, but a higher degree of expression altogether. There was something frigidly impersonal about many of the C major Masses written for the cathedrals and monastery churches of Austria. After studying the old, yellowed manuscript parts of innumerable forgotten mid-eighteenth century Austrian composers in such monastery archives as Göttweig, Heiligenkreuz, Klosterneuburg or Lambach one is left with a curious and rather disturbing impression of impersonality. The endless trumpets

G

and drums in stereotyped half-baroque patterns, the almost obligatory "Cum Sancto Spiritu" and "Et vitam" fugues recur in work after work. But about 1770 the new spiritual renaissance makes itself felt not only in instrumental but also in church music; and we find a distinct tightening of the form and an increased personal expression in the masses of Gassmann, Hofmann and Haydn written at this time. Haydn's *Missa Stae. Caecilae*, written about the year 1773, is by far the finest church music he had hitherto composed: the serene, majestic "Kyrie" introduction, the sonorous baroque polyphony of the "Gratias," the flaming inspiration of the "Et vitam" fugue, the sombre C minor "Benedictus" —all these are the results of the new stylistic change.

Up to this point we have deliberately concentrated upon Vienna and its composers. But in the Austrian provinces there was a strong and venerable musical tradition, which in some cases (*e.g.* Graz. Innsbruck) stretched back into the centuries. One of the chief centres of ecclesiastical music was the Princely Archiepiscopal Court of Salzburg, where, in the baroque period, music had flourished. In fact, not even Vienna approached the staggering size and the rich pomp of the Mass in Fifty-Three Parts (twelve choirs of voices and instruments) by Orazio Benevoli (1605–1672), written for the consecration of the Salzburg Cathedral in 1628. The antiphonal tradition prevailed until well into the second half of the eighteenth century, and Leopold Mozart writes to his son, on 1 November 1777, of the first performance of the *Missa Sancti Hieronymi* by Johann Michael Haydn, Joseph's brother:

"This very moment I have returned from the Mass at the Cathedral, where they performed the [Hieronymus] Mass by Haydn: he conducted it himself. He also wrote the Offertorium and instead of the Sonata he composed the Graduale [in Salzburg it was customary to play a Sonata for Organ and Orchestra instead of the proper Graduale] . . . I liked it all very much, because six oboes, three double-basses, two bassoons and the castrato [Ceccarelli]—who has been engaged at a monthly salary of 100 florins for a half a year—assisted. [Leopold then explains the antiphonal disposition of the forces and adds:] . . . What I particularly liked was that the oboes and bassoons closely approach the human voice, and the Tuttis seemed to be pure and full vocal music since the sopranos and altos were reinforced by six oboes and the alto trombones, and therefore equalled in size and strength the mass of tenor and bass voices; the pieno was so majestic that I could have done without the oboe solos. The whole business lasted an hour and a quarter, but it was too short for me, for it was really brilliantly written . . .".

The *Hieronymus Mass* was written for the Salzburg Archbishop of the same name. Apparently Michael Haydn had forgotten (or ignored) the new rule which the Archbishop had made the year preceding: that the long fugues at the end of the Gloria and Credo must be omitted, and that the whole service must not last longer than forty-five minutes. Hieronymus said of the new work (to quote Leopold Mozart again) that "Haydn did not seem to have understood what he (the Archbishop) wanted . . . but since Haydn had begun in this way the Archbishop had decided not to say anything more, in order not to confuse and irritate him."

This tact which the Archbishop showed to Haydn places him in a far more friendly light than in the Mozart literature. But the fault undoubtedly lies on both sides, for Wolfgang Mozart was certainly a difficult young man, to say the least. Concerning the new rule of 1776, we have an interesting letter of Wolfgang, written to the famous Italian theorist, Padre Martini, with whom the Mozarts had come in contact on their Italian sojourns. Mozart writes, on September 4 1776:

"Our church music is very different from that of Italy, since a mass with the whole Kyrie, Gloria, Credo, Epistle sonata, Offertorium or Motet, Sanctus and Agnus Dei must not exceed three quarters of an hour. This applies even to the most solemn Mass held by the Archbishop himself. So you see that a special study is necessary for this sort of composition. At the same time, the Mass must have all the instruments, trumpets, drums and so forth . . ."

The limitation of Salzburg's church music was not only one of duration, however, but also of style. Like the Viennese, the Salzburg school continued to write its church music in the strict style, or *stile osservato*, though Italian influences continued to prevail. For this reason there is a certain stiffness and archaic quality in many of Mozart's masses written for the Archiepiscopal Court: we feel that his music is somewhat constricted, slightly impersonal. Recently I heard in Salzburg performances of a series of C major Masses in the K. 200s (the so-called *Spatzenmesse*, K. 220, is the best known) and was again struck by their stiff, traditional character. Of course we find moments of great genius (such as the magical tenor solo entrance in the "Quoniam" of K. 220); but one feels strongly that Mozart was standing beside himself, as it were; that he has divorced his emotional self from the music he is writing: and this is most curious in a composer who is surely the perfect combination of emotion and intellect. Yet even in the church music of this pre-Mannheim period, we find a distinct line of artistic develop-

K.273

ment, within the self-imposed limits of the *stile osservato:* K. 257–259 undoubtedly have more personal features than K. 220, which shows Mozart's church music at about its worst. In particular, the brilliant and festive "Credo" Mass of 1776 (K. 257) has a stunning impact. The last and certainly most beautiful of the pre-Mannheim church music is a Motet, *Sancta Maria* (K. 273), written on September 9, 1777, one day before the Feast of the Nativity of the Virgin Mary. "This wonderful piece," writes Einstein (*Mozart*, London, 1946 p. 341) "stands between the *De profundis* of 1771 (K. 93) and the *Ave verum* of 1791; it has in common with the latter the fact that it is written for the same forces—a four-part chorus, strings, and organ. And it is perhaps the peer of the *Ave verum*. It is songlike and at the same time a work of consummate skill; it is as profound as it is simple; it preserves humility in the presence of the divine and awe in the presence of the inscrutable, and it is full of trust and purity of feeling—one might say, full of intimacy. And one can scarcely listen to it without thinking of the stage it represents in Mozart's life—youth, the joy of youth is gone; the disappointments of the journey through life begin."

With the long trip through Germany to Paris, Mozart renounced forever the trite church music of his earlier years. The unfinished Mass (Kyrie in E flat, K. 322) shows what Mozart could have written in Mannheim in the way of a Mass without the Archbishop's restrictions of length and style. But even upon his return to Salzburg, an embittered but fully mature composer, he showed immediately that the days of the *Spatzenmesse* were finished. The first Mass upon his return was the so-called "Coronation Mass," supposedly written in honour of the miraculous image of the Virgin Mary at the Church of Maria Plain, near Salzburg (K. 317, March 1779). It is without question the first great Mass Mozart wrote, full of brilliance and depth, and uniting the newly orchestral style with the traditional form of the mass. The trumpets and kettledrums fulfil a new function here—not just the cold, neo-baroque fanfares of earlier days. There are no strict fugues, but there is a marvellous passage at the end of the "Credo", where the voices enter in swift imitation.

This work is followed by the "stormy solemnity" of the *Vesperae de Dominica* (K.321), a "Kyrie" fragment (K.323), a *Regina coeli* (K. 276), and by the magnificent *Missa Solemnis* in C (K. 337) written, a year after the "Coronation Mass." K. 337 is the last Mass written for the Archbishop. It is truly a "solemn" mass, full of that ambiguous major-minor use of C major which we find in the Symphony, K. 338, and with a severe, almost frighteningly *osservato* Benedictus, in A minor. The orchestra (indeed the whole texture) is thoroughly symphonic, and the whole piece is imbued with a towering strength, a complete assuredness of style. The quiet close of the "Dona nobis pacem" is almost unique in Salzburg church music (it reminds one of the similar close in Joseph Haydn's *Missa brevis Sancti Joanni de Deo*, written about five years earlier). What must the Archbishop have thought of this brilliant, stern, rebellious music?

The same year (1780) Mozart wrote a *Vesperae solennes de confessore* (K. 339): again music combining depth and brilliance. The concluding "Magnificat" is close to the sombre C major solemnity of the Mass, K. 337. "With this work [the Vespers]," writes Einstein (*op. cit.*, p. 345), "Mozart's ecclesiastical activity for Salzburg came to its inner as well as to its external conclusion. It had become so free, so personal, that it alone would sooner or later have led to a break with the Archbishop— for let no one think that Colloredo, who had occasion to hear the works of other masters also, especially Michael Haydn's, was deaf to the subjectivity or musical rebelliousness of his Court Organist."

The link between Salzburg and Vienna was Munich, where Mozart produced his opera, *Idomeneo*, early in 1781. There he wrote a striking *Kyrie* in D minor (K. 341), with an exceptionally large orchestra, including two flutes, two oboes, two clarinets, two bassoons, four (!) horns, two trumpets, kettledrums, strings with viola (which was not generally included in Salzburg church music) and organ. It is clear that the turbulent and dramatic music of *Idomeneo* must have had its effect on neighbouring compositions, especially on this Kyrie. The choruses in *Idomeneo* are among the very finest and most original pieces in the opera; and indeed the stark power of "O voto tremendo" (with its muted trumpets and *timpani coperti*) is very close to the lean chromaticism of this *Kyrie*. Why he composed it, and whether it forms the beginning of a projected Mass, is now shrouded in mystery; but whatever outward stimulus Mozart may or may not have received, it occupies a position of central importance in Mozart's church music. Even its outward garb, the key of D minor (also the key of the *Requiem*), shows how far removed it is from the earlier Salzburg church music, of which all except two early works are in major keys. The profundity, the strong personal stamp, continue from the late C major masses of 1779 and 1780; but the late D minor *Kyrie* is still more serious, more urgent in its expression.

Although Mozart had no official church music to write in Vienna,

one of his first major works was a new and large Mass, in C minor (K.
427): it is clear that he wrote it from inner need. Outwardly it was
planned as a kind of votive offering for Constanze, whom he married
in August, 1782. With this work we again return to the mainstream of
the Viennese classical Mass, the history of which we have interrupted
in order that Mozart's sudden emergence on the scene should be prepared by some details of his earlier Salzburg period. Mozart wrote only
two large-scale church works in his Viennese period, the above mentioned Mass in C minor and the *Requiem;* but both occupy central
positions in the history of the Viennese classical Mass, and without
considering them (particularly the Mass in C minor) any judgment of
this great period in musical history would be incomplete.

In 1782 Mozart began work on his greatest piece of church music,
the C minor Mass, K. 427. To understand its significance (if not its
greatness, which is obvious from the first bars of the Kyrie), we must
return for a moment to the point at which we left the Viennese classical
Mass—about the beginning of the 'seventies. Between the *Missa
Sanctae Caecilae* of *c.* 1773 and 1782, Haydn wrote two masses, the
Missa brevis Sancti Joannis de Deo (*c.* 1775) and the *Missa Cellensis*
("Mariazellermesse" of 1782); in these two works we can trace to some
extent many of the trends in Viennese church music during the decade
from *c.* 1772 to *c.* 1782. In the first, the *Missa brevis*, Haydn rebels
against the pompous C major style and scores for solo soprano, choir,
two violins, bass (cello) and organ solo; the key, moreover, is B flat
major. And it is not only the size of the forces which is in strong op-
position to the Cathedral Mass (as one might call it), but also the whole
character of the work. The "Little Organ Mass," as it is called in
Austria and Germany (because of the solo part allotted to the organ in
the Benedictus) has that peculiar strength so often found in a miniature
art of all kinds. The Benedictus is a casket of rich design and ornamentation. Even finer is the miraculous transition that occurs at the
words "Dona nobis pacem"; this is one of these rare and blessed inspirations which will at times direct an artist; the stern, inflexible
"Agnus Dei" is suddenly transformed and transfigured, and a rare
serenity and peace descends on the music. It is typical that this lovely
metamorphosis is accomplished by purely chamber-musical means. At
the end, all voices and instruments die away (autograph: *perdendosi*),
leaving a quiet spirit of benediction never approached in any other
Mass by Haydn. It was essential for him to do away completely with
the stiff, trumpet-and-drum facade, and to write church music purely

from the heart—even in a manner closer to the string quartet than the mass or symphony.

The *Missa Cellensis* of 1782 reconciles the new popular instrumental style with the polyphonic tradition. The Viennese *motivische Arbeit* is wedded to the *stile osservato*, while in the Gratias we find strong traces of the delicate, chamber-musical approach of the *Missa brevis*. It is the first Viennese classical Mass which fully reconciles (1) the new intellectual sonata form, (2) the popular melody designed to delight the simple Austrian peasant, perhaps resting in the cool church at Mariazell after his long pilgrimage (*cf.* the *Vivace* of the Kyrie), and (3) the baroque splendour of C major, of trumpets and drums, of fugal and contrapuntal grandeur. It was a Mass which could only have come out of Vienna.

It was at this point that Mozart began his huge cantata-mass in C minor. But the qualities we have associated with Haydn's "Mariazellermesse" are intensified in Mozart's new work: intensified in that the "Kyrie" contains a real thematic development which rises to a climax of tremendous power; intensified, too, in that Mozart had experienced not only the fugal tradition of his predecessors in Salzburg and Vienna but also a greater heritage, namely, the knowledge of Bach's and Handel's music. He had the opportunity to study the great oratorios of Handel, and *Art of Fugue* and the *Well-Tempered Clavier* of Bach, at the house of Gottfried van Swieten; and the impact of this great baroque music on Mozart's style was indeed profound. Consequently we find in the C minor Mass enormous fugues, including (*e.g.* Osanna) those for double chorus: the structure of the "Cum Sancto" fugue at the end of the Gloria bears unmistakably the stamp of Bachian and Handelian grandeur, while the "Qui tollis" chorus (with 8-part choir) has the massivity of *Israel in Egypt*. Many of the arias, duets and terzets of the "Gloria" are also strongly baroque, baroque in the true sense, not neo-baroque in the manner of the earlier Cathedral Masses. The "Laudamus," on the other hand, is almost Italian in feeling. But at the same time there is a constant attempt to weave into these baroque patterns the symmetry of the Viennese melody and the intellectual aspects of Viennese sonata form (the development of motifs, the extension of thematic patterns, etc.). Not only this, we find in the exquisite "Incarnatus" the same chamber-musical delicacy of the Haydn *Missa brevis*, flavoured by that inscrutable harmonic ambiguity which is so much a part of Mozart (we refer to the opening and closing *ritornelli*).

Between 1782 and 1791, Mozart wrote no more masses and only one small piece of church music at all (the *Ave verum*, K. 618, of 1791). In the intervening years he had found Freemasonry (the *Maurerische Trauermusik* is a dramatic expression of his preoccupation with Masonic elements); this and the ambivalent attitude which Mozart had to his Church (partly, no doubt, as the result of his dealings with the Salzburg Archbishop) were the reasons for this long gap in his church music productions—apart from the fact that he received no commissions in the field. From 1782 until after his return from London, Haydn also wrote no masses (or as far as we can tell any church music at all). This lack of large-scale Viennese masses was, however, due to the so-called *Josephinische Verbote*, a series of far-reaching reforms with which Joseph II sought to decentralize the power of the church in the Austrian Empire. Many monasteries were secularized, and the splendour of church services, including the performance of large masses with many instruments, was sharply curtailed. On 25 February, 1783 an edict was issued, in which simplified services were ordered, and in which it was made clear when services were to take place, which altars were to be used, which Ritual employed, and so forth. It was Joseph's plan to have a "chorale" service, in which the congregation took more part in the proceedings than hitherto. The general trend had been going on for some years, and we find a Berlin paper (*Die Vossische Zeitung*) of 1782 writing of Viennese church music as follows:

"In the Imperial Chapel the earlier kind of church music has been abandoned; the other churches will probably follow suit . . ."

and shortly afterwards:

"Vienna. In our seven parochial churches it is planned to have two sermons, held according to the Imperial Reform which is already in practice; instrumental and florid music is now completely absent from the churches, except on high festival days . . ."

In a series of further edicts, instrumental masses were specifically limited. On 19 April, 1784 a detailed law was put into force (we cite from J. A. Petzek, *Sammlung politisch-geistlicher Gesetze für die V. Oe.Lande*, 2 vols., Freiburg 1795–1796, No. 212):

"In those churches in which a proper chorus is maintained, the *Segenmesse* shall be read at seven or eight o'clock in the morning, according to the time of the year, and apart from this a choral mass, with or without organ but without instrumental music, shall be sung.

"The High Mass will be given in towns and Cities on Sundays and holidays with instrumental and/or choral music, if one or the other has been in general use hitherto; but in the country it shall be held with such ceremony only on those days in which it is required that the monstrance be shewn to the people: on all other Sundays and holidays, however, the normal German chorale mass shall be sung to the *Segenmesse*, with the organ [only] . . .

"The Vespers shall be sung daily with the usual chorales, on important holidays with an organ, but without instrumental music . . ."

This state of affairs prevailed until the death of Joseph II, in 1790. Of course instrumental masses were to be heard now and then in Vienna, in the main provincial towns (such as Salzburg), and of course in the larger Austrian monasteries (*e.g.* Lambach, Melk, Kremsmünster, Göttweig, Stams)—all of which did not take the edicts too seriously. Their archives show very clearly that instrumental masses were in fact written and performed in this period of *Josephinische Verbote*. But one wonders whether Mozart would have been commissioned to write a Requiem Mass, and whether Haydn would (or could) have written his last six masses, if Joseph II had reigned into the next century.

If Mozart had continued to live, he would (as we now know) have succeeded to the post of Chapel Master of St. Stephen's Cathedral in Vienna; he would have assisted Haydn in producing the final quintessence of the Viennese classical Mass. As it was, Haydn was fated to carry on the tradition alone, in a series of magnificent late works (1796–1802), after which Beethoven and Schubert, amid a host of lesser figures such as Hummel, Gyrowetz and Diabelli, brought this great era to its close; at the same time, of course, they also opened new vistas into the nineteenth century, to the masses of Liszt, Bruckner and other Austrian Romantics.

Mozart's *Requiem* stands on the threshold of this final period. His church music of the year 1791 (which includes the exquisite *Ave verum* mentioned above), and Haydn's final masses, *Te Deum* and the two late oratorios (*Die Schöpfung* and *Die Jahreszeiten*) are the golden harvest—the late autumn gathering—of a proud and noble tradition in vocal and instrumental music. This church music contains the distillation of much that had been written before; Haydn had received a great stimulus from Handel's oratorios in England, so that both he and Mozart received anew the spiritual force of the baroque; but added to this was the wealth of Viennese instrumental music, to the development and perfection of which Haydn and Mozart themselves had contributed so much. The wonderfully mature fusion of these styles made possible not only Mozart's *Ave verum, Requiem* and Haydn's *Nelson Mass* but also Beethoven's *Missa solemnis* and the Ninth Symphony.

The Roman Catholic Requiem Service

For those readers who may wish to know something of the purpose and form of the Roman Catholic service for the dead, the following brief notes may be of assistance. The Requiem Mass differs from the normal Mass (apart from the obvious difference of its function) in that the whole service is intended to be sung by the choir and, moreover, remains fixed, *i.e.*, it does change according to different circumstances. It will be remembered that, in the normal Mass, the Introitus, Graduale, Offertorium and Communio change according to the period of the Church Year, and that only the Kyrie, Gloria, Credo, Sanctus, Benedictus and Agnus are fixed. Composers (*e.g.* Michael Haydn) may have written the proper Graduale and Offertorium for a Mass to be performed on a certain festival day; but usually composers wrote just the six movements, by which the work was not limited to any one feast. The Graduale, Tractus, Sequence and Offertorium of the *Missa pro defunctis* (Requiem), on the other hand, remain fixed and do not change. Mozart's *Requiem* omits the Graduale, Tractus and part of the Offertorium ("Libera eas"); in liturgical performances one must, strictly speaking, add these in Gregorian chant. A table showing the difference between the Mass and Requiem may clarify matters:

Normal Mass	*Missa pro defunctis* *(Requiem)*
Introitus (changing)	⎰ "Requiem" and Kyrie
Kyrie	⎱ written in one section.
Gloria	(omitted because of the joyful character of the text).
Graduale, Tractus, Sequence (changing)	"Requiem," "Absolve," "Dies irae."
Credo	(omitted).
Offertorium (changing)	Offertorium "Domine"
Sanctus	Sanctus
Benedictus	Benedictus
Agnus	⎰ Agnus and "Lux aeterna"
Communio (changing)	⎱ written in one section.

As will be seen in the following text (see pp. 112ff, *infra*) of the *Missa pro defunctis*, Mozart divided the sequence, "Dies irae," into six independant sections, most of them short, but clearly interlocked: the progressive tonality of the "Rex tremendae" (from G minor to D minor) is typical of the interconnection which these separate sections manifest. The offertorium is divided in two sections ("Domine Jesu" and "Hostias"). Otherwise (apart from those sections omitted altogether) each part of the ritual is allotted one movement in Mozart's *Requiem*.

The Circumstances of Mozart's Requiem

In July, 1791 Mozart was in Vienna, while his wife, Constanze, took the cure in Baden, a favourite spa some three hours away. He was hard at work on *Die Zauberflöte* and on 2 July he writes:

". . . Please tell Süssmayer, that fatuous ass, to send me the score of the first act, from the introduction to the finale, so that I can orchestrate it."

Franz Xaver Süssmayer (1776–1803) was one of Mozart's pupils; he wrote most of the recitatives to the opera *La Clemenza di Tito*, and we shall see, he is intimately connected with the history of the *Requiem*.

About this time a mysterious grey-liveried messenger appeared at Mozart's flat. He announced that his anonymous master would like to have Mozart write a *Requiem*, and wished to know if he were disposed to do so, and what fee would be required. Mozart was already a sick man, and in his overwrought mind he began to imagine that this was an emissary of death, a messenger from the other world; but he accepted the commission, and the grey-liveried stranger returned with the proposed sum (in one contemporary report 50, in another 100 Ducats). The messenger cautioned Mozart not to try to discover the identity of the patron. Mozart actually began to work on the *Requiem*, and sketched out parts of the Introitus, the "Kyrie" fugue, and the sequence up to the end of the "Rex tremendae." But the sudden commission of *La Clemenza di Tito*, which Mozart wrote in less than three weeks, forced him to abandon work on the *Requiem* temporarily. *Tito* was performed in Prague on September 6, and upon his return to Vienna, Mozart had to finish *Die Zauberflöte*, of which he conducted the first performance in the *Freihaustheater auf der Wieden* on 30 September. In Prague Mozart was obviously very ill, for after his death, a letter from that city (12 December, 1791) notes that "he returned home

from Prague ill, and since then sank visibly . . . Because his body was
swollen in death, it is believed that he was poisoned."

In his hysterical state of mind, Mozart was indeed convinced that he
was being poisoned. The diaries of Vincent and Mary Novello, who
went to Salzburg to visit Constanze in 1829 and wrote down their
interviews with her, throw some light on this situation (*A Mozart
Pilgrimage, Being the Travel Diaries of Vincent and Mary Novello in the
year 1829*, transcribed and compiled by Nerina Medici di Marignano
edited by Rosemary Hughes, London, Novello, 1955):

[Mary Novello, 17 July, 1829] "Some six months before his [Mozart's]
death he was possessed with the idea of his being poisoned—'I know I must
die,' he exclaimed, 'someone has given me acqua toffana [a slow poison, said
to include arsenic and lead oxide, it was given in small doses, and the victim
died only after a considerable interval] and has calculated the precise time of
my death—for which they have ordered a Requiem, it is for myself I am
writing this.' His wife entreated him to let her put it aside, saying he was too
ill, otherwise he would not have such an absurd idea. He agreed she should
and wrote a Masonic ode [*Eine kleine Freymaurer-Kantate*, completed 15
November 1791] which so delighted the company for whom it was written
that he returned quite elated: 'Did I not know that I have written better I
should think this the best of my work . . . Yes I see I was ill to have such an
absurd idea of having taken poison, give me back the Requiem and I will
go on with it.' But in a few days he was as ill as ever and possessed with the
same idea."

[Vincent Novello, 15 July, 1829] "It was about six months before he died
that he was impressed with the horrid idea that someone had poisoned him
with acqua toffana—he came to her one day and complained that he felt
great pain in his loins and a general languor spreading over him by degrees—
that some one of his enemies had succeeded in administering the deleterious
mixture which would cause his death and that they could already calculate at
what precise time it would infallibly take place. The engagement for the
Requiem hurt him much as it fed these sad thoughts that naturally resulted
from his weak state of health.

". . . On one occasion he himself with Süssmayer and Madame Mozart
tried over part of the Requiem together, but some of the passages so excited
him that he could not refrain from tears, and was unable to proceed.

"I was pleased to find that I had guessed right in supposing that the 'Recordare' (one of the most divine and enchanting movements ever written) was one of his own greatest favourites.

"What glorious productions have been lost to the world by his unfortunate early death—for incomparable as his works are I have not the least doubt but that he would have written still finer things such as oratorios and other extensive works (of the epic class) had he lived."

As Mozart grew steadily more ill, he continued to work feverishly on the unfinished *Requiem*. On 4 December, (the day before he died), he is reported to have asked the score to be brought to his bed, and propped up, he and three friends (including Benedict Schack, the first Tamino) sang the "Lacrymosa." Later, Constanze told the Novellos that Mozart "called Süssmayer to him and desired that if he died before he had completed the work, that the fugue he had written at the commencement might be repeated and pointed out where and how other parts should be filled up that were already sketched." The following contemporary report, made by Mozart's sister-in-law, Sophie Haibl, gives an accurate and pathetic picture of Mozart's last illness:

"Now when Mozart became ill, we both made him a nightgown which he could take off from the front, because he could not turn in bed due to boils; and since we didn't know how really sick he was, we made him a nice padded dressing-gown, so that when he could get up, he would feel comfortable. And we visited him regularly, and he seemed very pleased about the dressing-gown . . . On the day before he died, he said to me: '*Ach* dear Sophie, good that you are here: you must see me die. I have even now the taste of death on my tongue. And who will look after my sweet Constanze if you don't stay here?' And then he said to Süssmayer: 'Didn't I tell you that I was writing the Requiem for myself?' "

After he and his friends had sung part of the *Requiem*, Mozart "sat up in bed and stared into space, then lay back and turned towards the wall and seemed to sleep." In his delirium he now imagined that he was in the *Freihaustheater* hearing the piercing high notes of his other sister-in-law, Josepha Lange, as the "Queen of the Night," then he seemed to be driven by the wild "Dies irae" of his *Requiem*. Sophie Haibl reports that she will never forget the fantastic scene of Mozart, blowing out his swollen, inflamed cheeks, trying to imitate the kettledrums in some part of the work. At 55 minutes after midnight on 5 December, he died in a coma, completely unconscious.

Constanze, beside herself with grief and hysteria, was put to bed. The next day the swollen, distorted body, was taken to the Cathedral, where at 3 o'clock the funeral service was held. Only a few mourners were present, and they followed the procession only part of the way to the cemetery of St. Marx, far outside the city walls. And from this moment, legend began to grow round the fantastic death. It is reported that the mourners had to turn back at the city gates because of wild snow and rain, and that Mozart, who died with terrible debts, was thrown into a mass pauper's grave. But a contemporary diary[1] recently examined, tells of "tems [*sic*] doux. Troi[s] ou quatre[s] brouillards par jour depuis quelque tems [*sic*]", for 5 December and "Tems [*sic*] doux. En brouillard frequent" for 6 December. Mozart's burial, as we now know, was by no means the cheapest; and his grave was certainly not a *Massengrab*. The truth of the matter is that Constanze, perhaps superstitious, did not attempt to find her husband's grave until many years afterwards (one might add, maliciously, not until he was very famous); and when she did go—which was probably on the urging of Nissen, whose mistress she then was—the grave-tender who had buried Mozart was no longer there, and no one could tell where he was buried.

The grey-clad emissary of the other world, as Mozart imagined him to be (how near the eighteenth century, was, despite its enlightenment, to the superstition of the middle ages!), was none other than the valet of one Count von Walsegg zu Stuppach, who liked to order works from professional composers and play them as his own. His wife had died on 14 February 1791, and he planned to perform Mozart's *Requiem* under his (Walsegg's) name.

After Mozart's death, the widow had the unenviable task of putting his disordered, debt-ridden financial affairs in order. She trembled at the thought that the unknown patron would demand the return of the fee, and decided to have one of Mozart's friends complete the work. And from this point on, there are details which only Mozart, Süssmayer, Eybler and Constanze could clarify; the exact history of how the *Requiem* came to be completed is no longer known, and was never entirely clear.

1). MS Tagebuch von Graf Zinzendorf [MS. diary of Count Zinzendorf], Vienna City Archives. See O. E. Deutsch, *Die Dokumente seines Lebens*, Kassel 1961, p. 367.

The extant MS. (in the Vienna National Library) shows that Mozart had finished the Introitus ("Requiem aeternam") and "Kyrie"; the "Dies irae" was completed in the vocal parts, the *basso continuo,* and certain key instrumental sections, while the "Lacrymosa" stopped at the first half-cadence. The Offertorium and its versicle ("Domine Jesu" and "Hostias") were in the same, half-finished state. Nothing of the Sanctus, Benedictus and Agnus existed.

Although Constanze reported (as we have seen) that her husband had given clear instructions to Süssmayer how the work was to be finished, she first turned to Joseph Eybler, a local composer of considerable repute, who began to fill in the missing parts. Why Eybler rather than Süssmayer was chosen is but one of the mysteries. Now recent examination of all the old copies and the autograph in the Vienna National Library has shown that Eybler's part in the completion is greater than was hitherto supposed. Moreover, Constanze appealed to other musicians to help, when Eybler decided not to continue (apparently Stadler and Albrechtsberger were among those whom Constanze asked, and who refused). So Süssmayer, far from being the logical first choice, was third or fourth. This lends credence to the theory that the whole death-bed conversation with Süssmayer was made up later, in order that people should imagine that Süssmayer had all sorts of sketches, verbal instructions, and so on, with which to complete the work. Constanze's later repudiation of Süssmayer's part in the work is very curious (see *infra*).

To return to Eybler: in 1933[2] the Vienna National Library acquired his score of the "Domine" and "Hostias," from which it is clear that Süssmayer simply took Eybler's version and incorporated it almost without change (he simplified Eybler's more complex figured bass). Moreover Eybler filled in some of the missing parts of Mozart's autograph: those parts in the facsimile edition (edited by Alfred Schnerich, Vienna, 1913) which are ringed in pencil are his. Although Süssmayer seems to have copied Eybler's version of the "Domine" and "Hostias," he did not use Eybler's version of the missing orchestral parts from the "Dies irae" up to the "Lacrymosa."

What Süssmayer did was to use Mozart's own autograph of the Introitus and Kyrie. Then he copied out all the parts extant in Mozart's handwriting and filled in the orchestration. (We shall deal with the

---

2). According to Haas (*Mozart*), p. 155.

final three movements later.) This procedure would, of course, have been suspect to Walsegg immediately if Süssmayer's handwriting had not been almost exactly like Mozart's (to this day, scraps of Süssmayer's autographs are sold as Mozart's!) One wonders why he did not use Eybler's very satisfactory orchestration. In fact there are points of Süssmayer's version which are definitely inferior to those of Eybler.

Ex. 1

The Mozart Requiem, "Dies irae", bars 52 - 56, in the reconstruction of Joseph Eybler.

In the "Dies irae," for example, Eybler filled in the trumpet and drum parts in a far more Mozartean way than did Süssmayer: the former has those pungent dotted rhythms which we find so often in Mozart, whereas the latter has the Haydenesque rhythmic figure of bar 32 leading to repeated quavers in the trumpets which are most unlike Mozart's use of these instruments:

Ex. 2

The Mozart Requiem, same passage, in Süssmayer's reconstruction

The vital question now arises; just what is the extent of Süssmayer's participation in the *Requiem*? Here is a table showing the state of the autograph as we now have it (the added parts in Eybler's hand are not considered here):

Introitus ("Requiem aeternam")	completed.
Kyrie fugue	completed.
From "Dies irae" to "Lacrymosa"	vocal parts, basso continuo, most of the violin I and some fragments of the other instruments completed.
"Lacrymosa"	bars 1–8 ditto (breaks off at this point).
"Domine Jesu," "Hostias"	ditto.
Sanctus, Benedictus, Agnus	completely lacking.

One point in our earlier section, concerning Mozart's last days, should be mentioned: Benedict Schack (see *supra*) reports that he sang some of the "Lacrymosa" on Mozart's death bed[3]. But only the first eight bars are extant in Mozart's handwriting. Were there more sketches, or notes, showing how the movement should be completed? Or is Schack's report perhaps an error? And what of the last three movements, which Süssmayer said he wrote entirely? The theme of the "Benedictus" was found in a batch of Mozart's sketches, and again, there may have been instructions, verbal and written. Modern scholarship thinks that Süssmayer's participation is less than was once believed: but Wilhelm Fischer has convincingly shown that the end of the "Lacrymosa" could be improved (see *Mozart-Jahrbuch* 1951), and almost all writers (Einstein, Haas, *etc.*) have objected to the "crude trombone writing." The extant documents on the subject are included below; we reproduce them as they are, without comment; the reader can make up his own mind, for scholarship has never discovered the true secret, and never will.

Before listing these documents, however, we must complete the

3). Deutsch *op. cit.*, p. 460. Recently, an interesting sketch to the *Requiem*, in Mozart's hand, was discovered—one not used by Süssmayer. See *Neue Mozart Ausgabe*, Werkgruppe 1, Abteilung 2, Teilband 1, ed. by Leopold Nowak, Kassel 1965, pp. 60 f. See also Wolfgang Plath, "Über Skizzen zu Mozart's 'Requiem'" in: *Bericht über den Internationalen Musikwissenschaftlichen Kongress*, Kassel 1962 (1963), pp. 184 ff.

early history of the *Requiem*. Süssmayer completed his work, and Constanze delivered the MS. to the steward of Count Walsegg zu Stuppach (whose identity was not yet known to her). The Count performed the work on 14 December, 1793, at the church of the Cistercian Monastery "Neukloster" in Wiener Neustadt. But there had been semi-private performances before in Vienna, one arranged by Baron van Swieten "im Jahnschen Saale", 2 January, 1793. The diary of Count Zinzendorf (quoted in connection with Mozart's death) reports of the latter:

"Le soir chez la P[rince]sse Schwarzenberg, de là [*sic*] chez la vieille Princesse Colloredo ce qui m'a fait manquer le Requiem de Mozart."

It was generally known that Süssmayer had had a hand in the work, and after publication of the letter in the *Allgemeine musikalische Zeitung* (see *infra*), Count Walsegg, naturally annoyed, required an explanation. By this time, Constanze was the mistress of the Danish Legationssekretär, Georg Nikolaus von Nissen, and it was obviously he who decided to tell Stuppach the truth. Nissen went to him, accompanied by Abbé Stadler, an old family friend who had long assisted Constanze in selling her husband's manuscripts, making catalogues, and so on. They told the Count what had happened, and admitted Süssmayer's part in the composition; the Count (who was obviously not in too happy a position either, since he had attempted to palm off the *Requiem* as his work) was disposed to forget the whole story.

The documents relating to Süssmayer's participation are *inter alia* the following:

[Letter from Constanze to Breitkopf and Härtel, 1799]

". . . As far as the Requiem is concerned, I certainly do have the famous one which he wrote just before his death. I know only this one Requiem, and do not hesitate to judge the others spurious. Exactly how much he himself wrote—and it is his, till near the end of the work—I shall explain to you when you receive it from me. The situation is as follows: when he saw that he would die, he spoke to Herr Süssmayer, the present Imperial Chapel Master, and asked him that, should he really die without finishing the piece, the first fugue (which is very useable anyway) be repeated in the last section; [Mozart] told him, moreover, how he should fashion the end of the work, of which the main part was already written down, at least here and there, in parts. And Herr Süssmayer really did do just that."

But Breitkopf & Härtel were apparently still suspicious and required a further statement from Süssmayer, which he furnished on 8 February 1800, and which Breitkopf & Härtel printed in their house magazine, *Allgemeine musikalische Zeitung*, in October of the following year:

"I owe too much to the teaching of this great man to allow me to be silent when a work, which is largely of my composition, is to be published as his, for I am convinced that my part is unworthy of this great man. Mozart's compositions are so unique, and I dare assert that they so far surpass those of almost all living composers, that any imitator, especially with direct falsifications, will fare much worse than the magpie who donned a peacock's feathers. The completion of the Requiem, which has been the subject of our correspondence, was given to me through the following circumstances. Mozart's widow could well imagine that the posthumous works of her husband would be in great demand, and death took him as he was working on the Requiem. Various masters were asked to complete it; some could not accept because of pressing engagements, while others did not wish to put their talents beside those of Mozart. Finally, I was given the task, because it was known that I had played through and sung those parts of the work which he had completed in his lifetime, that he had often spoken to me of its completion, and had explained the process of, and reasons for, his instrumentation. I can only hope that I have at least had the fortune to have done my work in such a way that those who know Mozart will here and there find some traces of his unforgettable teaching. In the "Requiem" and "Kyrie", "Dies irae" and "Domine Jesu Christe", Mozart had completed the four vocal parts and the figured bass, but in the scoring had only indicated a point here and there. In the "Dies irae", the last line set by him was 'Qua resurget ex favilla'; and his scoring was the same as in the previous sections. From the line 'judicandus homo res' onwards I completed the "Dies irae." The Sanctus," "Benedictus" and "Agnus Dei" were all newly fashioned [*ganz neu . . . verfertiget*] by me; I have only taken the liberty of repeating the fugue at the line 'Cum Sanctis', etc., to give the work more unity. I shall be very happy if I have shown you a small service by this statement."

Süssmayer (perhaps innocently) made an incorrect statement when he said that the "Requiem" and "Kyrie" were incompletely orchestrated. And the term "*ganz neu . . . verfertiget*" can be taken to mean either "newly composed" or "newly fashioned" (*i.e.*, from extant material): we have preferred the latter translation; but if Süssmayer did have sketches for these three movements, he neglects to inform his readers of the fact. Mary Novello (*op. cit.*, p. 126) says of this document that Constanze "justly observed [that] any one could have written what he [Süssmayer] had done, after the sketching and precise directions of Mozart, and nothing Süssmayer ever did, before or after, proved him to have any talent of a similar kind."

One can easily cavil at this or that point in Süssmayer's instrumentation; but as Fischer has aptly said, his version is the one that is "dear and close to us," and the most we may dare to do is to alter a detail or two. Whatever criticisms have been levelled at Süssmayer, however, it is obvious that he was steeped in the style of the *Requiem*, and finished it in a reverent way. It is like the unfinished tower of St. Stephen's Cathedral in Vienna: the builders did not intend it to be unfinished, but time has decreed that it remain so, and to change it would be to destroy a view which is "dear and close to us."

Analytical and Descriptive Notes

Mozart's *Requiem* has several general stylistic features which give it a very personal quality. The choice of key, D minor is typical; we find it earlier in Mozart's career, for instance in the string Quartet K. 421, in the famous Piano Concerto, K. 466, and in some of the best parts of *Idomeneo* and *Don Giovanni*. It is a key which Mozart treats quite differently from G minor, for instance. Whereas G minor often has a desperate note in Mozart, D minor is treated more sternly on the one hand (*cf.* the Piano Concerto, *Don Giovanni*, and the "Dies irae" of the present work), and more tenderly and poignantly on the other (*cf.* the quartet and the present "Lacrymosa"). G minor is perhaps more intimate, more personally connected with Mozart's self, while D minor is used for tragedy on the grand scale: this is why we find the catastrophic operatic scenes in *Idomeneo* and *Don Giovanni* written in the latter, while the catastrophic personal conflict (*e.g.*, String Quintet, Symphony K. 550: Finale) finds its outlet in the former.

The scoring is also characteristic. In order to give a leaner, more acid orchestral sound, Mozart bans the flutes and horns from the orchestra, much as Haydn was to do in his great D minor work, the "Nelson Mass" (1798). But instead of retaining oboes, Mozart has chosen the milder basset horns, and thus the two main emotional features of the *Requiem*—dramatic strength and pity—are contained in the instrumental accompaniment. The tender, mild emotion of the

"Recordare" is largely the result of the intertwining, liquid basset horn parts—oboes would not have been half so effective. The inclusion of trombones (unusual in much Viennese church music) shows Mozart's Salzburgian musical background.

The style itself bears a strong similarity to most of Mozart's earlier Mass in C minor, K. 427. The fugues are baroque, and many of the rhythmic figures derive from the past. The nineteenth century, for instance, rather objected to what they considered the neo-baroque "Kyrie" fugue, based on an age-old figure with a characteristic diminished-seventh leap:

Ex. 3

We find this figure in Handel's *Messiah* ("And with his stripes"), in Haydn's Quartet in F minor, Opus 20, No. 5—Finale (1772), and in Mozart's own early string Quartet, K. 168—*Andante* (1773). Perhaps even more striking is the dotted rhythm of the "Rex tremendae" opening, which (taken by itself) could be from a French overture of 100 years earlier:

Ex. 4

And its extension is, if anything, still more in the baroque tradition:

Ex. 5

No one not knowing the *Requiem* would guess that Ex. 5 was from a Mozart composition of the year 1791!

As for the entrance of the voices in this same movement, could it be that Mozart saw the beginning of Bach's *Passion According to St. John* when he was in Leipzig two years ealier? The similarity, even to the key, is certainly striking:

Ex. 6

J. S. Bach : Passion According to St. John, First Chorus

Ex. 7

Mozart : Requiem, " Rex tremendae ", entrance of the Chorus

Robert Haas (*Mozart*, Potsdam, 1933 /1950, p. 155) has shown that the beginning of the work is based on Florian Leopold Gassmann's *Requiem* in C minor; and one can also find an early example in Handel's *Funeral Ode* for Queen Caroline:

Ex. 8

Florian Leopold Gassmann: Requiem in C minor—Introitus

Ex. 9

Mozart : Requiem - Introitus, bar 34 *ff.*

But the progression in itself is based on the *dux-comes* relationship of the fugue form (I subject, V answer) and is—apart from the Gassmann model—probably just another example of the *Requiem's* baroque harmonic, thematic and emotional lay-out.

The Introitus, however, contains one very significant feature: the use of a Gregorian melody for the entrance of the words, "Te decet hymnus, Deus in Sion." The age-old heritage of the church is thus combined with the severe polyphony that Mozart chose to use in this work. Incidentally, the use of Gregorian chants in Viennese classical music is more frequent than was hitherto believed. We find them in many works by Haydn (*e.g.*, *Sinfonia Lamentatione* No. 26 in D minor, the "Alleluja" Symphony No. 30, the *Nelson Mass*, the late *Te Deum*—even in wind-band divertimenti); but also in music of Mozart's Salzburg precursors, *e.g.* in Ernst Eberlin's (1702–1762) Oratorio, *Der blutschwitzende Jesus*, where we have the late medieval Passion music, also found in Mozart's *Maurerische Trauermusic* and Haydn's *Sinfonia Lamentatione*. The stirring "Te decet" melody appears in the solo soprano in B flat:

Ex. 10

Te de - cet hy - mnus De - us in Si - on   et ti - bi re- de- tur vo-tum in Je- ru - sa- lem

At this point it would seem appropriate to introduce an extremely interesting model which Mozart obviously knew: the *Requiem* in C minor by Haydn's brother Johann Michael, who, as we have seen, was Mozart's colleague at Salzburg. This Michael *Requiem* is a powerful and moving piece of music, rather severe and scored with a lean acidity (trumpets, trombones, kettledrums, strings, organ, bassoon *col basso*). There are no soft instruments, not even oboes. The four trumpet parts are used very strangely: stiff, biting, almost piercing, they scream out in the *clarino* register and cut across the sombre C minor texture like a knife: the Haydn brothers have one thing in common in that their orchestration is never, or seldom in their earlier years, beautiful *per se*. Michael does not make one compromise in the sound of this work: it is grey, forbidding, austere. One thinks at once of Joseph's *Sinfonia La Passione*—wholly different music but with the same lack of interest in a work sounding enticing. In this respect, both are at opposite ends of the artistic scale from Mozart, who as he often said, always wanted his music to please the ear.

The real sensation of this *Requiem* is that it is indisputably the direct model for Mozart's own *Requiem* written twenty years later. The similarities are too profound to be accidental: alone the Gregorian "Te decet hymnus" of both works makes one draw one's breath. This is hardly the place to enter into a detailed discussion of the many musical ideas in Michael's work which reappear in Mozart's; but I think a few words about the psychological motives may not be amiss. Why did Mozart, sick and slightly hysterical, return to this choral work of his respected Salzburg colleague? I am not a professional psychologist; but I feel very strongly that the explanation must lie in the strong link between life's three most important phases: birth, puberty, death. In 1771, Mozart was in his puberty, and the death of the Archbishop, who had been a real friend and patron to the Mozart family, must have come as a profound shock: and inextricably connected with this shock must have been the performance of Michael Haydn's powerful *Requiem*. It was the end of a whole *Lebensabschnitt* for Mozart. Now we must imagine the composer, twenty years later, asked to write a Requiem in mysterious circumstances which, strange enough in themselves, upset the nervous and sick man even more than would have been the case otherwise. He begins to write the great *Requiem,* and in his fevered fantasy, and deep from the swirling unconscious of a genius who retained every piece of music he ever heard (the more if he admired it, naturally), the strains of Michael's grim and unrelenting work must have risen to the surface and become intertwined with his own creative urge. The great emotional experience of puberty returns, spectre-like, to accompany, even to inspire much of the structural background of the new *Requiem.*

Contrary to the Mass in C minor (K. 427), the *Requiem* contains no florid solo arias; but like Haydn's *Missa Cellensis* (1782) it contains passages for solo vocal quartet, a practice which became standard in the late Viennese mass. The solo quartet is used for whole movements (Nos. 3 and 5) and also in the middle of choral movements (Nos. 8, 11) to serve as a colouristic contrast. (For this reason the lonely solo soprano in the Introitus—Ex. 10—is especially effective.)

The "Dies irae," a swift choral movement of terrific force, bursts upon us without orchestral ritornello (Haas thinks this, too, may be traced to Gassmann's above mentioned *Requiem*). The form, which compares to Mozart's big Elektra aria of *Idomeneo,* is most interesting; the second subsection approaches the recapitulation via C minor. Tonally, we have:

D minor—F major—A minor: A minor—C minor—D minor.

The lead-back to the recapitulation has a striking, sinewy series of quavers in the bass which is answered by the upper chorus:

See next page

Ex. 11

From this point onwards we find a fascinating and thematic motivic unity threading throughout the whole *Requiem*. Hans Keller's theory of latent unity in a work may be demonstrated easily in K. 626. We feel the musical and spiritual unity at once; analysis shows that our intuition is supported, as Robert Haas (*op. cit.*, p. 156) has shown, by countless motivic interrelationships. Keller writes (*Observer*, 29 April 1956): "A great work can be demonstrated to grow from an all-embracing basic idea, and variety is a necessary means of expressing a unity." In the case of K. 626 there are (as one would expect in such a large epic work)

several basic ideas. Following the Haas analysis, we find a clear relationship between the Introitus (Bass), the "Dies irae" (Bass line) and
the Agnus:

Ex. 12
(a) " Requiem aeternam " (Introitus), bars 8 - 9, Bass

(b) " Dies irae ", bars 1 - 5, Bass

(c) " Agnus ", bars 2 - 6, Bass

(*Cf.* also the bracketed portion of Ex. 13a, the soprano part of the
"Dies irae.") The soprano's opening bars of the "Dies irae" are also
clearly linked to those of the Sanctus:

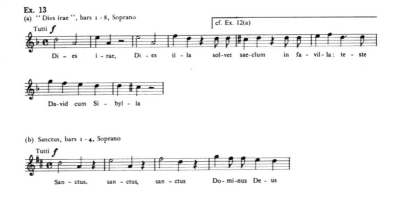

Ex. 13
(a) " Dies irae ", bars 1 - 8, Soprano

cf. Ex. 12(a)

(b) Sanctus, bars 1 - 4, Soprano

There are, moreover, thematic and motivic connections between the
second subject of the "Dies irae," at the words "Quantus tremor," and
the "Tuba mirum" (No. 3); between what Haas calls the "pseudo-
chromatic" line at the beginning of the third section of the "Dies

irae" (again "Quantus tremor") and the "Recordare" ("Ne me perdas," etc.), "Lacrymosa" ("parce Deus"), "Domine" ("ab ore leonis") and elsewhere. Among other things, there are clear ties between the "Lacrymosa" and Benedictus, and between the "Kyrie" fugue and the "Osanna" of Sanctus and Benedictus.

The "Tuba mirum" (No. 3) starts with a magnificent trombone solo, echoed by the solo bass:

Ex. 14

Unfortunately, Mozart carried the idea on a bit too long; such a passage as Ex. 15 is simply not well suited for the trombone (especially the chromatics); and Süssmayer continued to score for the solo trombone even after Mozart stopped (the stave is left blank after bar 19 or so). Einstein says, quite justifiably, that "this unquestionably Mozartean solo trombone is itself a painful matter—one cannot shake off the impression that the heavenly player is exhibiting his prowess instead of announcing the terrible moment of the Last Judgment" (*op. cit.*, p. 354).

Ex. 15

The stirring "Rex tremendae" has been mentioned above. There is a distinct relationship to the enormously powerful double chorus, "Qui tollis," in the C minor Mass: the little "Salva me" dotted figure towards the end reminds one of the same kind of soft interjection found in the "Qui tollis" chorus (we are thinking of the "miserere" passage). The "Recordare," which follows was as we have seen one of Mozart's favourite movements and seems to be characteristic of his attitude towards death. We must remember his letter to Leopold on the death of Wolfgang's dear friend the Count Hatzfeld:

(4 April 1787)

". . . As death, when we come to consider it closely, is the true goal of our existence, I have formed during the last few years, such close relations with this best and truest friend of mankind, that his image is not only no longer terrifying to me, but is indeed very soothing and consoling. And I thank my God for graciously granting me the opportunity (you know what I mean) of learning that death is the *ı ey* which unlocks the door to our true happiness. I never lie down at night without reflecting that—young as I am—I may not live to see another day."

The peaceful beginning of this movement with its gentle forward impulse of the semi-quavers is one of the finest parts of the work:

Ex. 16

A happy dualism gradually establishes itself in this movement—

a continual subject and answer: we see it in the "Quaerens me " which is divided between bass and tenor soli and taken as a group, the men are answered by the soprano and alto soli ("sedisti lassus" . . . "crucem passus"). This works into an even tighter overlapping ("tantus labor non sit cassus"). Later the dualism is expressed by interval, the words "Ingemisco . . ." and "culpa rubet . . ." being answered in the lower registers, "tamquam reus . . ." and "vultus meus."

The "Confutatis" begins with a furious, rhythmic accompaniment and jagged dotted choral entries. The intervening *piano* sections ("Voca me") are clearly linked to the foregoing "Recordare" by the rhythmic figure of the accompaniment:

Ex. 17

At the words "Oro supplex" both this and the first rhythmic figures are dropped, and a flowing crotchet and minim choral texture is supported by gentle syncopations in the accompanying strings. Undoubtedly the gradual subsiding of rhythmic turbulence is part of the preparation for the "Lacrymosa," which is probably the most sublime single part of the *Requiem*. The "Confutatis" was in A minor and ends with an inverted dominant seventh chord of D minor, the key of the "Lacrymosa." This may have been the last movement Mozart wrote; at any rate, the autograph is extant for only the first eight bars: but what eight bars they are! The *crescendo* to the half cadence with the chorus at first in short notes, gradually lengthening out to full dotted crotchets, is one of Mozart's greatest colouristic strokes of genius. Süssmayer's completion (if it is in fact his and not Mozart's) is, with the exception of a few doubtful choral entries, masterly; and whether he or Mozart wrote the final plagal cadence, it is one of the greatest moments in all music.

The "Domine Jesu" (No. 8) is a light-textured *Andante con moto* which leads to a stormy *fugato* on a typically baroque chromatic descending subject (Ex. 18):

Ex. 18

Ne ab - sor - be-at e - as tar - ta-rus, ne ca-dant in ob - scurum.

I

This is broken off after the exposition, and the solo quartet enters. There then follows the famous "quam olim Abrahae" fugue, on a tightly syncopated theme (Ex. 19). Somehow this always reminds me of the "Omnes, omnes generationes" fugue from Bach's *Magnificat* (that section of which happens to be in the same key, G minor). Perhaps it is because both enter rather suddenly, and because both have the same inexorable, intensely rhythmic forward drive, though the Bach generates its force by repeated quavers attached to and supported by semiquavers, while the Mozart is stamped by the off-beat entries of the main subject.

Ex. 19

The "Hostias" is a stately (*Andante*) three-four movement in E flat; as in the previous movement ("Domine Jesu"), Süssmayer has wisely allowed the trumpets and drums to be silent. In the "Hostias" he also begins without trombones, by which procedure he gives us a (too brief) respite from the heavy, rather old-fashioned trombone writing. In this movement we again find the upper and lower-octave choral dualism previous noticed in the "Recordare," to which this movement is spiritually (and motivically) related. At the end, the "quam olim Abrahae" fugue is repeated: Novello reports Stadler as saying that the direction to repeat this section was the last thing Mozart put on paper before he died.

Süssmayer's "Sanctus" begins wonderfully (*Adagio*). The chorus enters supported by the wind instruments, drums and *basso continuo;* the upper strings enter in the second half of each bar with a brilliant, golden wash of colour. The timpani part, incidentally, may be based on a similar figure in the Sanctus of Bach's Mass in B minor, which was known in Vienna towards the end of the eighteenth century (Haydn, for instance, owned a manuscript copy):

Ex. 20

At the words "Osanna" the tempo quickens to *Allegro* and a short fugato begins:

Ex. 21

It has often been asserted that the "Sanctus," as a movement, is far too short compared with the rest of the work. Only someone ignorant of the Viennese classical tradition could make such a criticism, for the Sanctus was always a very short movement, even in large, cantata-like masses, such as Haydn's *Missa Stae. Caeciliae.* In fact all Haydn's, Gassmann's, Reutter's, Leopold Hofmann's and other contemporary Viennese composers' Sanctus movements are extremely brief, partly because of the nature of the Catholic ritual at this most holy point in the Mass, and partly because it was Vienna's musical tradition.

The Benedictus, as we have seen, was based on a Mozart sketch. Like many of Haydn's late quartets and masses, the movement is in the flatted submediant major of the tonic major. Thus the tonal relationship of the last three movements is D (tonic major: Sanctus)—B flat (flatted submediant major, or if you will, the normal submediant of the tonic minor)—tonic minor (Agnus); the key of B flat is, therefore, a convenient pivot from tonic major back to tonic minor. The movement, like those of most Viennese classical masses, is allotted to the four solo voices and the tutti enters only with the *da capo* of the "Osanna." The first three bars will give the main theme and also an idea of Süssmayer's scoring, which is very Mozartean (notice the viola part in bar 3), except for the heavy, inept trombones, which Mozart would certainly not have used here:

Ex. 22

A typical "leading rhythm," marked *ff*, appears at the end of the first and last sections (here the trombones should have been introduced and not before). It is one of the best passages in the "Benedictus" and is strongly reminiscent of the atmosphere (and orchestration) of *Die Zauberflöte*:

Ex. 23

The return of the "Osanna" fugue in B flat is not Süssmayer's happiest inspiration, and one wonders if it had not been better to modulate to D major.

The "Agnus" begins with a moderately slow introduction, to which Süssmayer has tacked on the music of the "Introitus"; the Gregorian "Te decet" melody is now, somewhat incongruously, set to the words "Lux aeterna." But the key scheme is rather clever. Süssmayer starts in D minor, modulates to the relative major (F), which acts as the pivot (dominant) to B flat, at which point Mozart's music again enters from the point in the "Introitus" where B flat had been reached ("Te decet"). The rest of the work then duplicates the Introitus and "Kyrie" fugue, to which Süssmayer has set the words, "Cum sanctis tuis in aeternum." It is a compromise, of course; but a compromise which at least allows the *Requiem* to end with Mozart's music.

Imperfect as Mozart's last, unfinished work is, its position in his *oeuvre*, and in the history of music, is assured. We may charitably forgive its (and Süssmayer's) faults for the sublime and unforgettable moments; the old Haydn, after all was right: he said that Mozart's eternal fame would be secured if he had written nothing else except the *Requiem*.

Vienna, May 1956.

9. The Decline and Fall of Wolfgang Amadeus Mozart

A PROGRAMME FOR THE CANADIAN
BROADCASTING CORPORATION, 1967

Narrator: In March 1781, Wolfgang Amadeus Mozart was summoned by his patron, the Prince Archbishop of Salzburg, to go to Vienna, where the Archbishop had taken up temporary quarters in the palace of the Teutonic Knights. Relations between the haughty Archbishop and the temperamental young composer were not happy. Mozart, during the last two years in Salzburg, had become the greatest composer in Europe except for Joseph Haydn. But living in provincial Salzburg, hardly anyone knew of his music and his greatness. Mozart was restless—and difficult. He was twenty-five.

Vienna was fast becoming the musical capital of the world. Many of the Austro-Hungarian aristocratic families retained an orchestra and a resident composer; some had private opera houses in the country estates. There were two Court opera houses in Vienna, the Burgtheater and the Kärntnerthortheater, and under the benevolent rule of the Emperor Joseph II, both German and Italian opera flourished. The Italians, whose leader was the composer Salieri, formed a clique and bitterly resisted anyone who attempted to invade their sacred precincts, especially an Austrian. They intrigued Haydn's opera *La vera Costanza*, commissioned by the Vienna opera five years before Mozart's arrival, right out of town. Haydn had to give up and staged his new opera at Eszterháza Castle. But Haydn lived most of the year away from Vienna, and the Italian clique soon found a better object for their hate: the newcomer Mozart, who attempted to do everything—be a piano player, give symphonies, write operas, perform concertos.

The standard of music in Vienna was extremely high. The long-forgotten art of counterpoint was still cultivated here, and wedded to the new symphonic or quartet forms. Mozart will have soaked up the latest music, such as this Haydn symphony, which had just been circulated round the Austrian capital. Haydn was to be, in fact, the primary influence musically on Mozart's life.

Music: Haydn Symphony No. 70; Finale from bars 27 to 143 incl.

Narrator: Mozart was soon deep in his Viennese career, and in ever more serious trouble with his Archbishop. His letters to his father Leopold in Salzburg graphically describe all this:

Mozart:
Vienna, 24 March 1781
What you say about the Archbishop is to a certain extent perfectly true—I mean, as to the manner in which I tickle his ambition. But of what use is all this to me? I can't subsist on it.
    . . . Well, my chief object here is to introduce myself to the Emperor in some becoming way, for I am absolutely determined that he shall get to know me. I should love to run through my opera for him and then play a lot of fugues, for that is what he likes.
    . . . You know that there is a society in Vienna which gives concerts for the benefit of the widows of musicians, at which every professional musician plays gratis. The orchestra is a hundred and eighty strong. No virtuoso who has any love for his neighbour, refuses to give his services, if the society asks him to do so. Besides, in this way he can win the favour both of the Emperor and of the public.
Postscript 26 March, 1781
    I can now add that the Archbishop has given me permission to play at the concert for the widows.

Mozart:
Vienna, 4 April 1781
    I can say with truth, that I was very well pleased with the Viennese public yesterday, when I played at the concert for the widows in the Kärntnerthor Theatre. I had to begin all over again, because there was no end to the applause. Well, how much do you suppose I should make if I were to give a concert of my own, now that the public has got to know me? But this arch-booby of ours will not allow it P.S.—I assure

you that this is a splendid place—and for my métier the best one in the world. Everyone will tell you the same. Moreover, I like being here and therefore I am making all the profit out of it that I can. Believe me, my sole purpose is to make as much money as possible; for after good health it is the best thing to have.

Vienna, 9 May 1781

Mon très cher Père! I am still seething with rage! and you, my dearest and most beloved father, are doubtless in the same condition. My patience has been so long tried that at last it has given out. I am no longer so unfortunate as to be in Salzburg service. Today is a happy day for me. Just listen: Twice already that—I don't know what to call him—has said to my face the greatest *sottises* and *impertinences*, which I have not repeated to you, as I wished to spare your feelings, and for which I only refrained from taking my revenge on the spot because you, my most beloved father, were ever before my eyes. He called me a rascal and a dissolute fellow and told me to be off. And I endured it all, although I felt that not only my honour but yours also was being attacked. But, as you would have it so, I was silent. . . . When I entered the room his first words were:

Archbishop: 'Well, young fellow, when are you going off?' *I:* 'I intended to go tonight, but all the seats were already engaged.' Then he rushed full steam ahead, without pausing for breath—I was the most dissolute fellow he knew—no one served him so badly as I did—I had better leave today or else he would write home and have my salary stopped. I couldn't get a word in edgeways, for he blazed away like a fire. I listened to it all very calmly. He lied to my face that my salary was five hundred gulden, called me a scoundrel, a rascal, a vagabond. Oh, I really cannot tell you all he said. At last my blood began to boil, I could no longer contain myself and I said, 'So Your Grace is not satisfied with me?' 'What, you dare to threaten me—you scoundrel? There is the door! Look out, for I will have nothing more to do with such a miserable wretch.' At last I said: 'Nor I with you!' 'Well, be off!' When leaving the room, I said: 'This is final. You shall have it tomorrow in writing.'—Do not send any more letters to the Deutsches Haus, nor enclose them in their parcels—I want to hear nothing more about Salzburg. I hate the Archbishop to madness.

Narrator: And shortly afterwards the ignomony was made complete.

Mozart: Instead of Count Arco accepting my petition, or getting an audience for me, enfin, no! He threw me out the door and gave me a kick in my behind!

Narrator: And so Wolfgang Amadeus Mozart was kicked down the stairs, out of the Archbishop's service—and into immortality.

Music: Piano Concerto in D, K. 451, first movement (good recording: Serkin/Schneider/Columbia). Hold till piano enters, then fade and hold under.

Narrator: In the past weeks before his dismissal, he had already secured many friends among the Viennese aristocracy, and now he began a spectacular career as a pianist and composer. He soon had pupils from fashionable society. In the salons of the great baroque palaces of the Austrian nobility—the Trautmannsdorfs, the Ester-házys, the Schwarzenbergs, the Liechtensteins—Mozart contributed to the glittering elegance of eighteenth-century Vienna.

Music: Fade up the piano concerto and hold for one minute, then fade and out.

Narrator: The address Mozart now moved to was at the house of the Weber family, cousins of the composer Carl Maria von Weber who was not yet born. When Mozart had been in Mannheim he had fallen in love with the eldest daughter, Aloysia. When he returned from Paris, expecting to find a loving girl-friend, he discovered that Aloysia had completely lost interest in him. Meanwhile the family had moved to Vienna. Leopold disliked the whole family intensely and was horrified when he read:

Mozart: Just address your letters: To be delivered at the House of the Eye of God on St. Peter's Square, in the second floor.

Narrator: Leopold protested violently, and Wolfgang tried to paint the Webers in the best light he knew. He had his good reasons for doing so.

Mozart:

Vienna, 16 May 1781

What you say about the Webers I do assure you is not true. I was a fool, I admit, about Aloysia Lange, but what does not a man do when he is in love? Indeed I loved her truly, and even now I feel that she is not a matter of indifference to me. It is, therefore, a good thing for me that her husband is a jealous fool and lets her go nowhere, so that I seldom have an opportunity of seeing her. Believe me when I say that old Madame Weber is a very obliging woman and that I cannot do enough for her in return for her kindness, as unfortunately I have no time to do so. Do not doubt, dearest and most beloved father, that everything will certainly turn out for my good and consequently for yours also. It is perfectly true that the Viennese are apt to change their affections, but only in the theatre; and my special line is too popular not to enable me to support myself. Vienna is certainly the land of the piano! And even granted that they do get tired of me, they won't do so for a few years, certainly not before then. In the meantime I shall have gained both honour and money.

Vienna, 15 December 1781

Dearest father! Oh, how gladly would I have opened my heart to you long ago, but I was deterred by the reproaches you might have made to me for thinking of such a thing at an unseasonable time—although indeed thinking can never be unseasonable. Meanwhile I am very anxious to secure here a small but certain income, which, together with what chance may provide, will enable me to live here quite comfortable—and then—to marry! You are horrified at the idea? But I entreat you, dearest, most beloved father, to listen to me. I have been obliged to reveal my intentions to you. You must, therefore, allow me to disclose to you my reasons, which, moreover, are very well founded. The voice of nature speaks as loud in me as in others, louder, perhaps, than in many a big strong lout of a fellow.

. . . But who is the object of my love? Do not be horrified again, I entreat you. Surely not one of the Webers? Yes, one of the Webers— but not Josefa, nor Sophie, but Constanze, the middle one.

. . . She is not ugly, but at the same time far from beautiful. Her whole beauty consists in two little black eyes and a pretty figure. She has no wit, but she has enough common sense to enable her to fulfil her duties as a wife and mother. It is a downright lie that she is inclined to be extravagant. On the contrary, she is accustomed to be shabbily dressed, for the little that her mother has been able to do for her children, she has done for the two others, but never for Constanze. True, she would like to be neatly and cleanly dressed, but not smartly, and most things that a woman needs she is able to make for herself; and she dresses her own hair every day. Moreover she understands house-keeping and has the kindest heart in the world. I love her and she loves me with all her heart. Tell me whether I could wish myself a better wife? One thing more I must tell you, which is that when I resigned the Archbishop's service, our love had not yet begun. It was born of her tender care and attentions when I was living in their house.

Narrator: Mozart soon excited the Emperor Joseph II's attention. Joseph, like most of the Habsburg family, was musical and fancied himself a connoisseur—but he really much preferred Dittersdorf to Haydn and Mozart. You couldn't exactly overlook Mozart, whose mercurial personality was fascinating the salons and concert halls of Vienna. But the Court treated him as something of a freak, to be exhibited like a tame monkey.

Mozart:
Vienna, 16 January 1782
Now a word about Clementi. He is an excellent cembalo-player, but that is all. He has great facility with his right hand. His star passages are thirds. Apart from this, he has not a farthing's worth of taste or feeling; he is a mere *mechanicus*. After we had stood on ceremony long enough, the Emperor declared that Clementi ought to begin. 'La Santa Chiesa Cattolica', he said, Clementi being a Roman. He improvised and then played a sonata. The Emperor then turned to me: 'Allons, fire away'. I improvised and played variations.
. . . He was very gracious, said a great deal to me privately, and even mentioned my marriage. Who knows? Perhaps—what do you think?

Mozart:
Vienna, 13 February 1782
My hair is always done by six o'clock in the morning and by seven I am fully dressed. I then compose until nine. From nine to one I give lessons. Then I lunch, unless I am invited to some house where they lunch at two or even three o'clock, as, for example, today and tomorrow at Countess Zichy's and Countess Thun's. I can never work before five or six o'clock in the evening, and even then I am often prevented

by a concert. If I am not prevented, I compose until nine. I then go to my dear Constanze, though the joy of seeing one another is nearly always spoilt by her mother's bitter remarks. For that is the reason why I am longing to be able to set her free and to rescue her as soon as possible. At half past ten or eleven I come home—it depends on her mother's darts and on my capacity to endure them. As I cannot rely on being able to compose in the evening owing to the concerts which are taking place and also to the uncertainty as to whether I may not be summoned now here and now there, it is my custom (especially if I get home early) to compose a little before going to bed. I often go on writing until one—and am up again at six.

Narrator: Mozart had been commissioned to write his first opera for Vienna, "Die Entführung aus dem Serail", "The Elopement from the Scraglio". Mozart's passion was opera and he devoted long months to the reworking of the libretto to suit his own view of what was good and bad in musical drama. The opera was a great public success, but Mozart's brilliance had begun to arouse the envy and hate of his colleagues.

Music: Finale from *Entführung* Act I "Ach Constanze". Hold for 2 minutes, then fade and hold under the next letter.

Mozart:
Vienna, 20 July 1782
Mon très cher Père! I hope that you received safely my last letter informing you of the good reception of my opera. It was given yesterday for the second time. Can you really believe it, but yesterday there was an even stronger cabal against it than on the first evening. The whole first act was accompanied by hissing.
. . . The theatre was almost more crowded than on the first night and on the preceding day no reserved seats were to be had, either in the stalls or in the third circle, and not a single box. My opera has brought in 1,200 gulden in the two days. I send you herewith the original score and two copies of the libretto.

Music: Bring up Finale Act I *Entführung* and run to end of Act.

Mozart:

Vienna, 27 July 1782

Dearest, most beloved father, I implore you by all you hold dear in the world to give your consent to my marriage with my dear Constanze. Do not suppose that it is just for the sake of getting married. If that were the only reason, I would gladly wait. But I realize that it is absolutely necessary for my own honour and for that of my girl, and for the sake of my health and spirits. My heart is restless and my head confused; in such a condition how can one think and work to any good purpose? And why am I in all this state? Well, because most people think that we are already married.

. . . Most beloved father, I am longing to have your consent. I feel sure that you will give it, for my honour and my peace of mind depend upon it. Do not postpone too long the joy of embracing your son and his wife. I kiss your hands a thousand times and am ever your obedient son W. A. Mozart.

Music: Serenade K. 361 for 13 wind instruments. Third movement. Adagio. After one minute, fade and hold under the following.

Mozart:

Vienna, 7 August 1782

I kiss your hands and thank you with all the tenderness which a son has ever felt for a father, for your kind consent and fatherly blessing. I was married by the blessing of God to my beloved Constanze. I was quite assured of your consent and was therefore comforted.

. . . When we had been joined together, both my wife and I began to weep. All present, even the priest, were deeply touched and all wept to see how much our hearts were moved. Indeed for a considerable time before we were married we had always attended Mass and gone to confession and received Communion together; and I found that I never prayed so fervently or confessed and received Communion so devoutly as by her side; and she felt the same. In short, we are made for each other; and God who orders all things and consequently has ordained this also, will not forsake us. We both thank you most submissively for your fatherly blessing.

Music: Bring up Adagio from Serenade and play to end.

Narrator: Leopold Mozart to the Baroness von Waldstaedten in

Vienna:
Leopold Mozart:
Salzburg, 23 August 1782

Highly born and gracious Lady! I thank your Ladyship most warmly for the special interest you take in my circumstances and for your extraordinary kindness in celebrating my son's wedding day with such liberality. When I was a young fellow I used to think that philosophers were people who said little, seldom laughed and turned a sulky face upon the world in general. But my own experiences have completely persuaded me that without knowing it I must be a philosopher. For having done my duty as a father, having in countless letters made the clearest and most lucid representations to Wolfgang on every point and being convinced that he knows my trying circumstances, which are extremely grievous to a man of my age, and that he is aware of the degradations I am suffering in Salzburg, since he must realize that both morally and materially I am being punished for his conduct, all that I can now do is to leave him to his own resources (as he evidently wishes) and pray God to bestow on him His paternal blessing and not withdraw from him His Divine grace. For my part I shall not abandon the cheerfulness which is natural to me and which in spite of my advancing years I still possess; and I shall continue to hope for the best. On the whole, I should feel quite easy in my mind, were it not that I have detected in my son an outstanding fault, which is, that he is far too patient or rather easy-going, too indolent, perhaps even too proud, in short, that he has the sum total of all those traits which render a man inactive; on the other hand, he is too impatient, too hasty and will not bide his time. Two opposing elements rule his nature, I mean, there is either too much or too little, never the golden mean. If he is not actually in want, then he is immediately satisfied and becomes indolent and lazy. If he has to bestir himself, then he realizes his worth and wants to make his fortune at once. Nothing must stand in his way; yet it is unfortunately the most capable people and those who possess outstanding genius who have the greatest obstacles to face. Who will prevent him from pursuing his present career in Vienna if he only has a little patience?

Mozart:
Vienna, 29 March 1783

Mon très cher Père! I need not tell you very much about the success of my concert, for no doubt you have already heard of it. Suffice it so say that the theatre could not have been more crowded and that every box was full. But what pleased me most of all was that His Majesty the Emperor was present and, goodness!—how delighted he was and how he applauded me! It is his custom to send the money to the box-office before going to the theatre; otherwise I should have been fully justified in counting on a larger sum, for really his delight was beyond all bounds. He sent twenty-five ducats.

Music: Rondo in D for piano & orchestra K. 382 (Complete).

Mozart: I go every Sunday at twelve o'clock to the Baron van Swieten, where nothing is played but Handel and Bach. I am collecting at the moment fugues of Bach—not only of Sebastian, but also of Emanuel and Friedemann. I am also collecting Handel's and should like to have the six I mentioned. I should like the Baron to hear Eberlin's too.

When the weather gets warmer, please make a search in the attic under the roof and send us some of your own church music. You have no reason whatever to be ashamed of it. Baron van Swieten and Starzer know as well as you and I that musical taste is continually changing—and, what is more, that this extends even to church music, which ought not to be the case. Hence it is that true church music is to be found only in attics and in a worm-eaten condition. When I come to Salzburg with my wife in July, as I hope to do, we shall discuss this point at greater length.

You will have seen from my last letter that I was to play at another concert. The Emperor was there too. I played my first concerto which I played at my concert. I was asked to repeat the rondo. So I sat down again; but instead of repeating it I had the conductor's rostrum removed and played alone. You should have heard how delighted the public were with this little surprise. They not only clapped but shouted 'bravo' and 'bravissimo'. The Emperor too stayed to hear me to the end and as soon as I left the piano he left his box; evidently he had only remained to listen to me.

Vienna, in the Prater, 3 May 1783
Mon très cher Père! I simply cannot make up my mind to drive back into town so early. The weather is far too lovely and it is far too delightful in the Prater today. We have taken our lunch out of doors and shall stay on until eight or nine in the evening. My whole company consists

of my little wife who is pregnant and hers consists of her little husband, who is not pregnant, but fat and flourishing.

Vienna, 7 May 1783

Well, the Italian opera buffa has started again here and is very popular. The buffo is particularly good—his name is Benucci. I have looked through at least a hundred libretti and more, but I have hardly found a single one with which I am satisfied; that is to say, so many alterations would have to be made here and there, that even if a poet would undertake to make them, it would be easier for him to write a completely new text—which indeed it is always best to do. Our poet here is now a certain Abbate da Ponte. He has an enormous amount to do in revising pieces for the theatre and he has to write per obbligo an entirely new libretto for Salieri, which will take him two months. He has promised after that to write a new libretto for me. But who knows whether he will be able to keep his word—or will want to? For, as you are aware, these Italian gentlemen are very civil to your face. Enough, we know them.

Narrator: In July 1783 Wolfgang and Constanze went to Salzburg. Mozart took with him the great C minor Mass in which he obviously wished to illustrate that church music should not be subject to changing fashion. In it, he also showed how profound had been the influence of Bach and Handel on him at those Sunday morning concerts given by Baron van Swieten. They performed the Mass in the ancient and severely beautiful abbey church of St. Peter in Salzburg, and Constanze, "la mia cara consorte", sang the soprano solo.

Music: Mass in C minor, Kyrie. After $1\frac{1}{2}$ minutes, fade and hold under.

Narrator: Salzburg was not a happy town for Mozart. They soon received the news that their little son Raimund had died in Vienna. Leopold and Nannerl, Mozart's sister, did not really warm to Constanze. The mood of the visit is caught in a curious episode that Constanze told many years later to an English woman, Mary Novello:

Woman Narrator: Constanze told me that their singing round the piano of the great Act 3 quartet from "Idomeneo", in which the young Idamante faces exile and disaster, wrought upon Mozart an over-

K

whelming and unaccountable wave of emotion. He burst into tears and quitted the chamber and it was some time before she could console him.

Narrator: It was as if he had a sudden premonition of the coming years.

Music: Bring up "Kyrie" from Mass in C minor and run to end of "Kyrie".

Narrator: Mozart returned to Vienna in November 1783 and entered the most brilliantly successful period of his life. He moved to a large and comfortable flat in the Singerstraße, just behind St. Stephen's Cathedral. Leopold came to visit the couple in 1785 and reported back to his daughter:
Leopold Mozart:
Vienna, 16 February 1785
We arrived at the Schulerstraße No. 846, first floor, at one o'clock on Friday. That your brother has very fine quarters with all the necessary furniture you may gather from the fact that his rent is 460 gulden. On the same evening we drove to his first subscription concert, at which a great many members of the aristocracy were present. Each person pays a souverain d'or or three ducats for these Lenten concerts. Your brother is giving them at the Mehlgrube and only pays half a souverain d'or each time for the hall. The concert was magnificent and the orchestra played splendidly. In addition to the symphonies a female singer of the Italian theatre sang two arias. Then we had a new and very fine concerto by Wolfgang, which the copyist was still copying when we arrived, and the rondo of which your brother did not even have time to play through, as he had to supervise the copying. You can well imagine that I met many acquaintances there who all came up to speak to me. I was also introduced to several other people.

On Saturday evening Herr Joseph Haydn and the two Barons Tinti came to see us and the new quartets were performed, or rather, the three new ones which Wolfgang has added to the other three which we have already. The new ones are somewhat easier, but at the same time excellent compositions. Haydn said to me: 'Before God and as an honest man I tell you that your son is the greatest composer known to me either in person or by name. He has taste and, what is more, the most profound knowledge of composition.''

Music: Quartet in A, K. 464, first movement. After two minutes fade and gradually fade completely during next paragraph.

Mozart: To my dear friend Haydn! A father who had decided to send out his sons into the great world, thought it his duty to entrust them to the protection and guidance of a man who was very celebrated at the time and who, moreover, happened to be his best friend.

In like manner I send my six sons to you, most celebrated and very dear friend. They are, indeed, the fruit of a long and laborious study; but the hope which many friends have given me that this toil will be in some degree rewarded, encourages me and flatters me with the thought that these children may one day prove a source of consolation to me.

During your last stay in this capital you yourself, my very dear friend, expressed to me your approval of these compositions. Your good opinion encourages me to offer them to you and leads me to hope that you will not consider them wholly unworthy of your favour. Please then receive them kindly and be to them a father, guide and friend. From this moment I surrender to you all my rights over them. I entreat you, however, to be indulgent to those faults which may have escaped a father's partial eye, and, in spite of them, to continue your generous friendship towards one who so highly appreciates it. Meanwhile I remain with all my heart, dearest friend, your most sincere friend W. A. Mozart.

Narrator: Leopold Mozart again reports on the events in Vienna:

Leopold Mozart:
On Sunday evening the Italian singer, Madame Laschi, who is leaving for Italy, gave a concert in the theatre, at which she sang two arias. A cello concerto was performed, a tenor and a bass each sang an aria and your brother played a glorious concerto, which he composed for Mlle Paradis for Paris. I was sitting only two boxes away from the very beautiful Princess of Wurtemberg and had the great pleasure of hearing so clearly all the interplay of the instruments that for sheer delight tears came into my eyes. When your brother left the platform the Emperor waved his hat and called out 'Bravo, Mozart.' And when he came on to play, there was a great deal of clapping.

We never get to bed before one o'clock and I never get up before nine. We lunch at two or half past. The weather is horrible. Every day there are concerts; and the whole time is given up to teaching, music, composing, and so forth. I feel rather out of it all. If only the concerts were over! It is impossible for me to describe the rush and bustle. Since my arrival your brother's fortepiano has been taken at least a dozen times to the theatre or to some other house. He has had a large fortepiano pedal made, which stands under the instrument and is about two feet long and extremely heavy. It is taken to the Mehlgrube every Friday and has also been taken to Count Zichy's and to Prince Kaunitz's.

Narrator: A great new plan was in the offing. Mozart was to write his first Italian opera for Vienna. When Leopold returned to Salzburg we hear of it, and how the director of the opera, Count Rosenberg, was pushing the pace:

Leopold Mozart: At last I have received a letter of twelve lines from your brother, dated November 2nd. He begs to be forgiven, as he is up to the eyes in work at his opera *Le Nozze di Figaro.* He thanks me and both of you for our good wishes and asks me particularly to make his excuses to you and to tell you with his love that he hasn't time to answer your letter at once. He adds that in order to keep the morning free for composing, he is now taking all his pupils in the afternoon, etc. I know the piece; it is a very tiresome play and the translation from the French will certainly have to be altered very freely, if it is to be effective as an opera. God grant that the text may be a success. I have no doubt about the music. But there will be a lot of running about and discussions before he gets the libretto so adjusted as to suit his purpose exactly. And no doubt according to his charming habit he has kept on postponing matters and has let the time slip by. So now he must set to work seriously, for Count Rosenberg is prodding him.

28 April 1786

Le Nozze di Figaro is being performed on the 28th for the first time. It will be surprising if it is a success, for I know that very powerful cabals have ranged themselves against your brother. Salieri and all his supporters will again try to move heaven and earth to down his opera. Herr & Mme. Duschek told me recently that it is on account of the very great reputation which your brother's exceptional talent and ability have won for him that so many people are plotting against him.

Narrator: Figaro was once again postponed, but the great evening was finally set for May 1, 1786. It was a brilliant success. At the third performance seven numbers were repeated, a duettino thrice. The Emperor Joseph II had to give orders to stop all arias from being encored. But *Figaro* was also the beginning of the aura of scandal that gradually began to surround Mozart. The play by Beaumarchais, "Le Mariage de Figaro", was a violently political satire and had been grimly forbidden by the Austrian court censors. The great librettist who managed to work his version past the steely eyes of the censor was Lorenzo da Ponte, but he was a famous debauché and carried with him his own aura of scandal. The alliance of da Ponte and Mozart was of course crucial to the development of opera but fatal to Mozart's social reputation. One Viennese newspaper wrote about *Figaro*, "What you can't say nowadays, you can hear sung". The aristocracy began to be slightly nervous about Mozart. Count Zinzendorf wrote in his diary after *Figaro*, "Mozart's music strange and without purpose".

Music: Le nozze di Figaro, Act III, the sextet (complete). Suggest use the Kleiber recording.

Narrator: Mozart felt that his future was not secure in Vienna, and he thought of joining the English group in Vienna when they returned to London. They included his pupil Thomas Atwood, the composer Stephen Storace, his sister Nancy Storace, Mozart's first Susanna, the tenor Michael Kelly, who sang Bartolo in the first *Figaro*, and the Storace's mother. Leopold, Wolfgang's father, was supposed to keep the children until Constanze and Wolfgang returned. Leopold considered this a presumption. He writes to his daughter:

Leopold Mozart: You can easily imagine that I had to express myself very emphatically, as your brother actually suggested that I should take charge of his two children, because he was proposing to undertake a journey through Germany to England in the middle of next carnival.
. . . Not at all a bad arrangement. They could go off and travel—they might even die—or remain in England—and I should have to run off after them with the children. As for the payment which he offers me for the children and for maids to look after them, well—Basta! If he cares to do so, he will find my excuse very clear and instructive.

Narrator: There was one place where he was still, to quote the local newspapers, "our great and beloved composer". The middle-class burghers of this city adored "Figaro" for musical *and* political reasons. Leopold Mozart reports to his daughter:

Leopold Mozart:
Salzburg, 12 January 1787
    Your brother and his wife must be in Prague by this time, for he wrote to say that he was leaving Vienna last Monday. His opera *Le nozze di Figaro* was performed there with such success, that the orchestra and a company of distinguished connoisseurs and lovers of music sent him letters inviting him to Prague and also a poem which was composed in his honour. I heard this from your brother, and Count Starhemberg heard about it from Prague.

    Narrator: On 15 January, Mozart writes to a friend in Vienna:

    Mozart: At six o'clock I drove with Count Canal to the so-called Bretfeldball, where the cream of the beauties of Prague is wont to gather. Why—you ought to have been there, my friend! I fancy I see you running, or rather, limping after all those pretty women, married and unmarried. I neither danced nor flirted with any of them, the former, because I was too tired, and the latter owing to my natural bashfulness. I looked on, however, with the greatest pleasure while all these people flew about in sheer delight to the music of my *Figaro.* arranged for quadrilles and waltzes. For here they talk about nothing but *Figaro.* Nothing is played, sung or whistled but *Figaro.* No opera is drawing like *Figaro.* Nothing, nothing but *Figaro.* Certainly a great honour for me.

    Music: Contretanz from K. 609, using "Non più andrai". (There is an old HMV 78 with Leo Blech; the Decca series have reached it by now).

    Mozart: I must frankly admit that, although I meet with all possible courtesies and honours here and although Prague is indeed a very beautiful and pleasant place, I long most ardently to be back in Vienna.

    Narrator: In December 1784, Mozart had taken a step which was to become vital to his life and philosophy. He had joined a Viennese lodge of the Freemasons, that ancient secret society dedicated to the brotherhood of man; here, among age-old symbols and comforting ritual, Mozart sought refuge from a society that was beginning to close its doors on him. Death somehow comes closer to Mozart. His father, Leopold, is now mortally ill.

Mozart:
Vienna, 4 April 1787
This very moment I have received a piece of news which greatly distresses me, the more so as I gathered from your last letter that, thank God, you were very well indeed. But now I hear that you are really ill. I need hardly tell you how greatly I am longing to receive some reassuring news from yourself. And I still expect it; although I have now made a habit of being prepared in all affairs of life for the worst. As death, when we come to consider it closely, is the true goal of our existence, I have formed during the last few years such close relations with this best and truest friend of mankind, that his image is not only no longer terrifying to me, but is indeed very soothing and consoling. And I thank my God for graciously granting me the opportunity (you know what I mean) of learning that death is the key which unlocks the door to our true happiness. I never lie down at night without reflecting that —young as I am—I may not live to see another day. Yet no one of all my acquaintances could say that in company I am morose or disgruntled. For this blessing I daily thank my Creator and wish with all my heart that each one of my fellow-creatures could enjoy it.

I hope and trust that while I am writing this, you are feeling better. But if, contrary to all expectation, you are not recovering, I implore you by God not to hide it from me, but to tell me the whole truth or get someone to write it to me, so that as quickly as is humanly possible I may come to your arms. I entreat you by all that is sacred—to both of us. Nevertheless, I trust that I shall soon have a reassuring letter from you; and cherishing this pleasant hope, I and my wife and our little Karl kiss your hands a thousand times and I am ever your most obedient son W. A. Mozart.

Music: Masonic Funeral Music K. 477. After fifteen seconds fade down and hold under to allow the following to be spoken, then bring up and continue to the end.

Mozart:
Vienna, 19 May 1787.

I inform you that on returning home today I received the sad news of my most beloved father's death. You can imagine the state I am in.

Music: up *Masonic Funeral Music* to end.

Narrator: The journey to Prague, and the enormous success of *Figaro*, bore fruit. Mozart was commissioned to write an opera especially for Prague: *Don Giovanni.* A letter to his friend Baron Gottfried von Jacquin tells of the opera's première:

Mozart:
Prague, 4 November 1787
Dearest, most beloved Friend! I hope you received my letter. My opera *Don Giovanni* had its first performance on October 29th and was received with the greatest applause. It was performed yesterday for the fourth time, for my benefit.

How I wish that my good friends were here just for one evening in order to share my pleasure! But perhaps my opera will be performed in Vienna after all. I hope so. People here are doing their best to persuade me to remain on for a couple of months and write another one. But I cannot accept this proposal, however flattering it may be.

Music: Don Giovanni. Bring in (Act II) the entrance of the statue very quickly after last speech and allow it to continue to end of scene (Don's going to hell).

Narrator: Mozart's friends were getting very worried about his precarious financial state. Perhaps Mozart's best friend, Joseph Haydn, put it all in a nutshell when he wrote to someone in Prague who had asked Haydn to write an opera for that city:

Haydn: If I could only impress on the soul of every friend of music, and on high personages in particular, how inimitable are Mozart's works, how profound, how musically intelligent, how extraordinarily sensitive! (for this is how I understand them, how I feel them)—why then the nations would vie with each other to possess such a jewel within their frontiers. Prague should hold him fast—but should reward him, too; for without this, the history of great geniuses is sad indeed, and gives but little encouragement to posterity to further exertions; and unfortunately this is why so many promising intellects fall by the wayside. It enrages me to think that this incomparable Mozart is not yet engaged by some imperial or royal court! Forgive me if I lose my head: but I love the man so dearly. I am, &c. Joseph Haydn.

Narrator: Finally the Emperor Joseph II decided to grant Mozart a yearly salary.

Mozart:
Vienna, 19 December 1787
Dearest Sister! I most humbly beg your pardon for having left you so long without an answer. Of my writing *Don Giovanni* for Prague and of the opera's triumphant success you may have heard already, but that His Majesty the Emperor has now taken me into his service will probably be news to you, I am sure you will be pleased to hear it.

Narrator: Mozart was engaged as Kapellmeister and Court composer to the Emperor on 1 December 1787. Mozart's salary was 800 gulden a year. Gluck just before him had received 2,000 gulden and Mozart's successor, the third-rate Kozeluch (Beethoven called him that "miserabilis") got 1,500. It soon turned out that Mozart's duties were limited to writing dance music for the official court balls, which took place in the stately Redoutensaal. On one receipt for his salary, Mozart wrote: "Too much for what I did, too little for what I could do." But even for the court balls, Mozart could not write second-rate music.

Music: German Dance K. 605, No. 3: bring in music at recapitulation, i.e. after F major sleigh-ride section with the sleigh-bells. Please use Bruno Walter recording if you have it.

Narrator: By 1788 Mozart was sinking into debt. His star was waning, and the Viennese aristocracy grew increasingly more suspicious of a composer who wrote political operas and music about libertines. Mozart's librettist tells of the reception of *Don Giovanni* when it was first performed at Vienna on 7 May 1788.

Da Ponte: The Emperor sent for me and told me that he was longing to see *Don Giovanni*. Mozart returned from Prague, and since Emperor Joseph was about to leave for military duties in the field, we hurried the score to the copyist to write out the parts. The opera went on the stage and . . . need I recall it? . . . *Don Giovanni* did not please! Everyone except Mozart thought there was something missing. Additions were made; some of the arias were changed; and it was offered for a second performance. *Don Giovanni* did not please! And what did the Emperor say? He said:

Joseph II: "That opera is divine; I should even venture that it is more beautiful than *Figaro*. But such music is not meat for the teeth of my Viennese."

Da Ponte: I reported the remark to Mozart, who said quietly:

Mozart: Give them time to chew on it.

Narrator: At a party given after the premiere of *Don Giovanni* there was a lot of comment and criticism. Suddenly the hostess noticed Joseph Haydn sitting on a sofa, listening to all the talk. The hostess went to Haydn and said:

Female Voice: But dear Haydn, we have not yet heard your opinion?

Haydn: I am not really qualified to judge the argument, but if you ask me, I think that Mozart is the greatest composer alive and *Don Giovanni* the greatest opera I know.

Narrator: Among Mozart's brother Freemasons, there were bankers and other wealthy men who were prepared to help Mozart. One of them was Michael Puchberg, also a friend of Haydn's.

Mozart:
Vienna, beginning of July 1788
Dearest Friend and Brother Freemason! Owing to great difficulties and complications my affairs have become so involved that it is of the utmost importance to raise some money on these two pawnbrokers' tickets. In the name of our friendship I implore you to do me this favour; but you must do it immediately. Forgive my importunity, but you know my situation. Ah! If only you had done what I asked you! Do it even now—then everything will be as I desire. Ever your Mozart.

Music: Adagio and Fugue K. 546: run through Adagio. Then stop for next letter.

Narrator: Mozart writes to a friend who has just joined the Freemasons.

Mozart:
Vienna, end of March 1789
Dearest Friend! I am taking the liberty of asking you without any hesitation for a favour. I should be very much obliged to you if you could and would lend me a hundred gulden until the 20th of next month. On that day I receive the quarterly instalment of my salary and shall then repay the loan with thanks. I have relied too much on a sum of a hundred ducats due to me from abroad. Up to the present I have not yet received it, although I am expecting it daily. Meanwhile I have left myself too short of cash, so that at the moment I greatly need some ready money and have therefore appealed to your goodness, for I am absolutely convinced of your friendship.

Well, we shall soon be able to call one another by a more delightful name! For your novitiate is very nearly at an end.

Music: Fugue of *Adagio and Fugue* K. 546.

Narrator: In 1789 Mozart was desperate. Would a journey abroad, to Germany, help his finances? He went to Dresden, Leipzig and Berlin. He writes back to Constanze, and these letters give us an intimate glimpse into his deep affection for his wife.

Mozart:
Dresden, 16 April 1789
Dear little wife, I have a number of requests to make! I beg you
(1) not to be melancholy,
(2) to take care of your health and to beware of the spring breezes,
(3) not to go out walking alone—and preferably not to go out walking at all,
(4) to feel absolutely assured of my love! Upto the present I have not written a single letter to you without placing your dear portrait before me.
(5) I beg you in your conduct not only to be careful of your honour and mine, but also to consider appearances. Do not be angry with me for asking this. You ought to love me even more for thus valuing our honour.

(6) and lastly I beg you to send me more details in your letters. I should very much like to know whether our brother-in-law Hofer came to see us the day after my departure? Whether he comes very often, as he promised me he would? Whether the Langes come sometimes? Whether progress is being made with the portrait? What sort of life you are leading. All these things are naturally of great interest to me.

Narrator: The visit did not bring the expected financial success. The King of Prussia was cordial to Mozart and he gave concerts; and there were offers to compose; but there was no cash at home when he returned to Vienna in the summer of 1789. Constanze had been ill, and Mozart was desperate.

Mozart:

Vienna, 12 July 1789

Dearest, most beloved Friend and most honourable Brother Free-mason! Great God! I would not wish my worst enemy to be in my present position! And if you, most beloved friend and brother, for-sake me, we are altogether lost, both my unfortunate and blameless self and my poor sick wife and child. Only the other day when I was with you I was longing to open my heart to you, but I had not the courage to do so—and indeed I should still not have the courage—for, as it is, I only dare to write and I tremble as I do so—and I should not even dare to write, were I not certain that you know me, that you are aware of my circumstances, and that you are wholly convinced of my innocence so far as my unfortunate and most distressing situation is concerned. Good God! I am coming to you not with thanks but with fresh entreaties! Instead of paying my debts I am asking for more money! If you really know me, you must sympathize with my anguish at having to do so. I need not tell you once more that owing to my un-fortunate illness I have been prevented from earning anything. But I must mention that in spite of my wretched condition I decided to give subscription concerts at home in order to be able to meet at least my present great and frequent expenses, for I was absolutely convinced of your friendly assistance. But even this has failed. Unfortunately Fate is so much against me, though only in Vienna, that even when I want to, I cannot make any money. A fortnight ago I sent round a list for subscribers and so far the only name on it is that of the Baron van Swieten.

Music: (must enter very suddenly): Symphony in G minor K 550, last movement, to enter at the beginning of the development (after double bar) and to continue through to end. Use Furtwängler recording if you have it.

Mozart:

Vienna, 17 July 1789

My wife was wretchedly ill again yesterday. Today leeches were applied and she is, thank God, somewhat better. I am indeed most unhappy, and am forever hovering between hope and fear. Dr. Closset came to see her again yesterday.

Narrator: Mozart's wife Constanze was sent off to Baden, half-a-day's carriage ride from Vienna, to take the cure. To compound Mozart's sorrows, he soon heard that Constanze was flirting scandalously at Baden. In the next letter, Constanze later erased the names, which we give as "N.N.".

Mozart:

Vienna, middle of August 1789

Dear little wife! I want to talk to you quite frankly. You have no reason whatever to be unhappy. You have a husband who loves you and does all he possibly can for you. As for your foot, you must just be patient and it will surely get well again. I am glad indeed when you have some fun—of course I am—but I do wish that you would not sometimes make yourself so cheap. In my opinion you are too free and easy with N.N. . . . and it was the same with N.N., when he was still at Baden. Now please remember that N.N. are not half so familiar with other women, whom they perhaps know more intimately, as they are with you. Why, N.N., who is usually a well-conducted fellow and particularly respectful to women, must have been misled by your behaviour into writing the most disgusting and most impertinent sotties which he put into his letter. A woman must always make herself respected, or else people will begin to talk about her. My love! Forgive me for being so frank, but my peace of mind demands it as well as our mutual happiness. Remember that you yourself once admitted to me that you were inclined to comply too easily. You know the consequences of that! Remember too the promise you gave to me! Oh, God, do try, my love! Be merry and happy and charming to me. Do not torment yourself and me with unnecessary jealousy. Believe in my love, for surely you have proofs of it, and you will see how happy we shall be. Rest assured that it is only by her prudent behaviour that a wife can enchain her husband. Adieu! Tomorrow I shall kiss you most tenderly.

Narrator: In an attempt to raise money, Mozart decided to issue several of his string quintets by subscription. His piano concertos had been successful that way a few years before. But times had changed and Mozart was going out of fashion.

Mozart: Since the number of subscribers is still very small, I am forced to postpone the delivery of my three quintets till 1 January 1789.

Narrator: Mozart received another commission for the Court Opera: he and Lorenzo da Ponte decided on *Così fan tutte.* The little group of Mozart's best friends, Haydn and Michael Puchberg, were there at the rehearsals. They realized what a supreme and profound masterpiece *Così* was, but the public was cool. *Così,* like its predecessors *Figaro* and *Don Giovanni* was a kind of scandal—not a political scandal; but it made an elegant, amusing thing out of wife-swapping. Many, too many, found the new opera frivolous and cynical. Conservative operatic goers in Vienna were obviously disturbed by Mozart's violently sensuous, indeed, erotic, and richly orchestrated music. In August 1790 *Così* was withdrawn and never given again in the composer's lifetime.

Mozart:
Vienna, 29 December 1789
    Most honourable Friend and Brother Freemason! Do not be alarmed at the contents of this letter! Only to you, most beloved friend, who know everything about me and my circumstances, have I the courage to open my heart completely. According to the present arrangement I am to receive from the management next month 200 ducats for my opera. If you can and will lend me 400 gulden until then, you will be rescuing your friend from the greatest embarrassment; and I give you my word of honour that by that time you will have the money back in full and with many thanks. . . .
    . . . Contrary to our arrangement we cannot have any music at our house tomorrow—I have too much work. But I invite you, you alone, to come along on Thursday at 10 o'clock in the morning to hear a short rehearsal of my opera. I am only inviting Haydn and yourself. I shall tell you when we meet about Salieri's plots, which, however, have

completely failed already. Adieu! Ever your grateful friend and brother W. A. Mozart.

Vienna, 20 January 1790

Dearest Friend! They forgot to deliver at the proper time your last kind note. So I could not reply to it sooner. I am very much touched by your friendship and kindness. If you can and will send me an extra hundred gulden, you will oblige me very greatly.

We are having the first instrumental rehearsal in the theatre to-morrow. Haydn is coming with me. If your business allows you to do so and if you care to hear the rehearsal, all you need do is to be so kind as to turn up at my quarters at ten o'clock tomorrow morning and then we shall all go there together.

Your most grateful friend, W. A. Mozart.

Music: Così fan tutte Karajan recording. Act I, Side two from beginning to end of Terzetto (the next secco begins: "Quante smarfie, quante buffonerie").

Narrator: Shortly after the premiere of *Così* the Emperor Joseph II died. He had been critical of Mozart at times but in a sense loyal to him as well. The new Emperor, Leopold II, was on the contrary deeply suspicious of Mozart and any hopes of regaining favour with the Court must have gone forever. Mozart went to the Imperial Coronation at Frankfurt where he gave a couple of concerts and hoped to draw attention to himself.

Mozart:
Frankfurt am Main, 15 October 1790

Dearest little Wife of my Heart! I have not yet received a reply to any of my letters from Frankfurt, which makes me rather anxious. My concert took place at eleven o'clock this morning. It was a splendid success from the point of view of honour and glory, but a failure as far as money was concerned. Unfortunately some Prince was giving a big *déjeuner* and the Hessian troops were holding a grand manoeuvre. But in any case some obstacle has arisen on every day during my stay here.

Narrator: In late November Mozart was back in Vienna. At far-away Eszterháza Castle, Haydn's great and magnanimous Prince had died, while Haydn was mounting Mozart's *Le nozze di Figaro*. Haydn went to Vienna and a few days later the door opened and in walked a man who said, "My name is Johann Peter Salomon. I have come from London to fetch you. Tomorrow we shall settle the contract." Salomon also came to fetch Mozart, but Mozart said he would follow along later. The day before Haydn and Salomon left, on 15 December 1790, they lunched with Mozart and the young composer wept. "We won't ever meet again", he said to Haydn.

1791 was to prove a highly productive year for Mozart. He composed all sorts of things—his last piano concerto, the beautiful clarinet Concerto in A and such an occasional but universal piece as the *Ave verum corpus*. The two principal works of the year were two new operas. Austria's new emperor Leopold II was to be crowned Bohemian King at Prague and the municipal authorities of that city asked Mozart to compose the music for the official Court Opera. The Court was dead against the idea but the Prague authorities insisted: They wanted Mozart and the new opera was entitled *La Clemenza di Tito*, a famous old libretto by Metastasio, which Mozart had to compose under great pressure. He dedicated the recitatives to his pupil Süssmayer. Mozart and his wife went to Prague for the final rehearsals. The Court, not being able to wreck the performance, did the next best thing: they arrived one hour late! The Empress hissed: "E' una porcheria tedesca" ("It's a bit of German swinishness!").

Music: Finale Act I *La.Clemenza di Tito*, last minute of the music.

Narrator: In the autumn Mozart was putting the final touches on another opera, *The Magic Flute*, and Mozart's wife was again at Baden, taking the cure. *The Magic Flute* on a text by Emanuel Schikaneder was commissioned by Schikaneder for his small theatre in one of the suburbs. Mozart's music was no longer fit for the Imperial Court Theatre. Mozart writes to his wife in Vienna in the night from 7 to 8 October, 1791:

Mozart: "I have just this moment returned from the opera which was as full as ever. As usual the duet "Mann und Weib" and Papageno's "Glockenspiel" in Act I had to be repeated and also the trio of the boys in Act III. But what always gives me most pleasure is the silent approval. You can see how this opera is becoming more and more esteemed."

Music: Die Zauberflöte, Act II, final chorus, last minute of the music.

Narrator: Mozart's financial situation continued to worsen, and it is hardly surprising that despite the success of the *Magic Flute*, Mozart was gradually falling prey to hysteria and despair. A mysterious stranger, clad in grey, appeared one day to commission a *Requiem*, and though in fact the stranger was only the servant of a Count who wished to pass off the work as his own, Mozart was terrified. He talked constantly of death. All the anguish of his life came out during a carriage ride one autumn day in 1791, in the beautiful Vienna Prater. He said to Constanze:

Mozart: Someone is poisoning me with *acqua toffana*. I feel a great pain in my loins. One of my enemies has succeeded in administering the poison and they've calculated the exact time of my death. I'm writing that *Requiem* for myself. But I don't want to die: life is so dear to me.

Music: Requiem (please use the old Jochum DGG recording made in the Vienna Cathedral in 1956): "Requiem aeternam" (1st movement): hold for one minute, then fade and hold under.

Narrator: Constanze Mozart later described her husband's state of mind.

Constanze Mozart: My husband became quite frantic and kept repeating: "I'm writing that Requiem for myself." I put him to bed and took the score away from him but when he grew slightly better again, he begged me to return the score, and so I did.

Music: Bring up *Requiem* for 15 seconds, then fade gradually under, allow following two speeches to begin, and fade completely.

Narrator: Sophie Haibl, Constanze's sister, was there during the final illness.

Sophie Haibl: I rushed away as fast as I could. Ah God, how shocked I was when my sister, half desperate but trying to keep herself under control, met me and said: "Thank God you're here, dear Sophie; last night he was so sick that I thought he wouldn't live to see the day. Do

L

please stay here, because if he's that bad again, he'll die this night. Go
and see how he is!" I tried to pull myself together and went to his bedside, and he called to me: "Ah, dear Sophie, good that you're here.
You must stay here tonight. You must see me die." I tried to make
myself strong and talk him out of it, but he said to me: "I've already
the taste of death on my tongue." And, "Who will look after my dear
Constanze if you don't stay here?" Yes, dear Mozart, but I have to go
to our mother and tell her that you would like to have me stay, otherwise she'll think something has happened to me. "Yes, do that, but
come back quickly!"—God, how I felt! My poor sister ran after me
and said, "For God's sake do go to the priests at St. Peter and ask a
priest to come as soon as he can!" I did that, but they refused to do for
some time, and I had a lot of trouble to get one of those priestly beasts
to go.—Then I ran to mother, who was anxiously awaiting me; it was
already dark. The poor thing was terribly shocked. I talked her into
going to her eldest daughter, the late Hofer, and to spend the night
with her, and that's what she did, and I ran back as quick as I could
to my inconsolable sister. Süssmayer was at Mozart's bedside; the
well-known *Requiem* was on the bed-spread and Mozart was explain-
ing to him how he ought to finish it after his death. He also told his
wife to keep his death secret until Albrechtsberger could be informed,
because that man deserved the post before God and man. The doctor,
Closett, was looked for all over, till they found him in the theatre; but
he had to wait till the piece was over—and then he came and ordered
cold compresses to be put on Mozart's feverish brow, and these pro-
vided such a shock that he did not regain consciousness again till he
died. The last thing he did was to imitate the kettledrums in his
Requiem, I can hear that even now. Then Müller from the Art Gallery
came and took a plaster cast of Mozart's white, dead face. I just cannot
describe to you, dear brother, how hopeless and pathetic his poor wife
was, she threw herself on her knees and prayed for help to the Almighty.
She couldn't leave him, as much as I begged her to; and if it were possible to increase her misery, it was in that the day after this frightful
night, great mobs of people came trapesing through, weeping and
sobbing . . .

Music: The section just before the "Lacrymosa" of the *Requiem*
begins—1 min., 20 sec. before "Lacrymosa" begins. Fade up and hold
under remaining speech.

Narrator: He died at fifty-five minutes after midnight on 5 December 1791. Constanze crawled into his bed and put her arms around him in the hopes of catching the fever herself. The next day his remains were blessed at the Crucifix-Chapel of St. Stephan's Cathedral; it was three o'clock in the afternoon, and it was damp and foggy. There was almost nobody there, and afterwards Mozart's body went unescorted, except for the burial personnel, on its last journey to St. Marx's cemetary, beyond the city walls, where Wolfgang Amadeus Mozart's last remains were placed in a grave. Later all the gravedigger could remember was that he lay somewhere near a flowering lilac tree.

Music: Bring up *Requiem* and play music to end of "Lacrymosa".

10. The "Jena" Symphony

(From the *Music Review*, 1957)

In 1909, Professor Fritz Stein discovered what he thought was an unknown early symphony by Beethoven. His source was a set of old manuscript parts in the archives of the Akademische Konzert in the university town of Jena; Beethoven's name appeared on the second violin ("Par Louis van Beethoven") and cello parts ("Symphonie von Bethoven [*sic*]"). Subsequently Stein edited a score of the work, which was published under Beethoven's name by Breitkopf & Härtel; he also wrote a long and interesting article on the find in volume XIII (1911–1912) of the *Sammelbände der Internationalen Musik-Gesellschaft* (hereinafter *SIMG*).

Critical opinion on the authenticity of the Symphony has been divided; some scholars, including Riemann, agreed with Stein, while many others remained sceptical. Stylistically the work is closely modelled on two Haydn symphonies, no. 93 in D (London, 1791) and especially no. 97 in C (London, 1792), as Stein points out in his preface to the score, and as Robert Simpson and the author have elaborated in some detail (see bibliography). The "Jena" Symphony, as it has come to be called, is not a great work, but it is certainly a good one, and a most interesting example of what composers—apart from Haydn —were writing in the 1790s.

Recently the following entry in the Göttweig Catalogue[1] caught the author's attention:

1). "Katalogus Operum Musicalum/in Choro musicali/Monasterii/O.S.P.B. Gottwicensis R.R.D.D./Altmanno/Abbate per R.D./Henricum/Wondratsch p.t. chori regentem, conscriptus/Anno MDCCCXXX", Vol. 11, p. 911.

"WITT discipulus celeb. Mozart[2] Capell/Mag[ister] Würzburg/ Symphonia/a 2 Violinis/2 Obois Flauto/2 Fagotti Viola/2 Corni e Clarinis/Tymp. Basso. [Left:] Comp [aravit] R P/Henricus 1825" followed by this theme (bass line has been omitted):

Ex. 1

As those who are familiar with the "Jena" Symphony will realize, the beginning of the Witt work is identical except for the first bar. I wrote at once to Göttweig, and learned that of the two symphonies by Witt listed in the catalogue—the other was in D major—by a fortunate chance this one was still extant; the Abbot of the Monastery, Dr. Wilhelm Zedinek, O.S.B., kindly brought the parts to Vienna, and it was at once obvious that we now have the "Jena" Symphony in contemporary manuscript parts under its real author. Textually, the Göttweig copy is far superior to that in Jena, and many of the doubtful points raised by Stein in his foreword are now explained. The absence of bar 1 in the "Jena" copy may well be a later change made by Witt himself; or it may represent the caprices of a local copyist.

Gerber's *Lexicon* (1814) is quite informative:

Witt (Friedrich) Grossherzogl[icher] Würzburgischer Hofkapellmeister, a talented and popular composer, born in Haltenbergstetten in Franconia in 1771, devoted himself to composition at an early age, and with great zeal. He was so successful that he soon found a post as cellist at the famous Princely Oettingen-Wallerstein Kapelle, and because of his great gifts he was given lessons in composition by the celebrated Rosetti, who was Kapellmeister there. He was a very diligent pupil and fulfilled his duties to the satisfaction of the entire court, and made such progress in composition that his works were heard gladly and with general applause at this most tasteful court. Even at Berlin, he performed an oratorio which he had written for King Friedrich Wilhelm II, and which was well received not only by the court but

2). There is no other evidence that Witt was a pupil of Mozart; indeed, it is most unlikely that the "disciplus celeb: Mozart" is meant literally.

also by the experts [*Kunstkenner*]. Later Herr Witt left the service of Prince Oettingen-Wallerstein and undertook many journeys through various countries, where his works were performed with great success, and where he wrote many new compositions. Finally in 1802 he wrote an oratorio for the Court Orchestra in Würzburg which was so favourably received that the then reigning Prince, Georg Karl, engaged him at once as Kapellmeister. In this capacity he wrote several masses and other pieces for the church, which were performed by the band of which he was director. The Grossherzog [who succeeded Georg Karl] confirmed the appointment, so that in 1807 he still continued to discharge his duties honourably.

He has written the following works: (1) *Die Auferstehung Jesu*, oratorio for the Royal Prussian Court, and performed in Berlin; (2) *Der leidende Heiland*, oratorio for the Court at Würzburg, performed there in 1802; (3) *Palma*, opera for the Frankfurt Theatre, performed there with success; (4) *Das Fischerweib*, opera, written in 1806 for the Grossherzogl. Hoftheater at Würzburg; (5) several cantatas of varying size; (6) several symphonies, of which six have been engraved at Offenbach from 1805 on; these works are favourites in our concerts; (7) several masses and pieces for the church; (8) *Concertante* for full orchestra, which work is considered in Würzburg to be the best of its kind in every respect; (9) various concertos for the cello, bassoon, flute, oboe, clarinet; numerous single and double horn concertos, *etc., etc.;* (10) various quartets and other works of this kind; (11) many pieces for wind band, variously scored. [Gerber adds:] Taken word for word from Dr. Siebold's *Nachrichten f. Fränkische Chronik*, 1807. Moreover, all this honourable and well merited praise of Herr Witt has been confirmed for some time by a holograph testimonial, which I own, written from Berlin by the late Türrschmiedt, an honest and experienced man. Recently the following works have been engraved: (12) Gr. Quintetto p. le Pf. Hautbois, Clarinette, Cor et Basson, et le même arrangé p. le Pf. 2 V. A. et Vc. Op. 6. Leipzig, b[ey] Breitkopf und Härtel, 1807; (13) Concerto p. la Fl. av. accomp. de l'orchestre. Ebend. 1807.

Fortunately, the excellent article by Ludwig Schiedermaier, "Die Blütezeit der Öttingen-Wallerstein'schen Hofkapelle" (*SIMG* IX, 1907–1908, pp. 83 *ff.*), is able to assist us in filling in Witt's biography. It appears that he was born on 8 November 1770 (not 1771), as Schiedermaier discovered by examining the parish records. His father, the *Kantor* Johann Caspar Witt, christened him as Jeremias Friedrich. A second son, Georg Friedrich, was born on 15 January, 1773, but it seems certain that the elder one is our man. Witt was engaged as cellist in the Oettingen-Wallerstein band on 21 January, 1790, with a salary of 300 fl. This date is important in view of what follows.

Joseph Haydn, who had been in contact with Prince Kraf[f]t Ernst of Oettingen-Wallerstein, paid a brief visit to the castle at Wallerstein in company with Johann Peter Salomon en route to England. He promised to pay a longer visit on his return trip. Whether he did or not cannot be established with certainty, but the author was able to find at the Oettingen-Wallerstein castle of Harburg authentic parts of several London symphonies, including nos. 93, 97 and 98. These copies were written by Haydn's factotum, Johann Elssler, and bear many holograph corrections and additions (see *Music Review* XV/1, 1954, p. 3 *et passim*). The young Witt was one of the first composers on the Continent to hear the new and sensational works which Haydn had written during his first English sojourn; thus we are able to trace exactly how symphonies nos. 93 and 97 made such a strong imprint on the "Jena" Symphony.

Together with the Bohemian clarinettist Josef Beer, Witt made concert tours to Potsdam in 1794 and Vienna in 1796. On 24th March, 1794, Türrschmiedt, who was also Gerber's informant, as we have seen, writes to Ignaz von Beecké (1733–1803), the Musikintendant at Wallerstein: "Witt's symphonies were very well received here [in Potsdam] . . .". This letter is valuable in that it shows us that Witt had written symphonies as early as 1794. Two years later Witt himself writes from Vienna to an unknown friend at Wallerstein:

We are comfortably settled, and who wouldn't be happy here? For there are amusements of every conceivable kind in abundance; there is even a concert at the Augarten every Saturday at 7 in the morning. The day before yesterday I gave one of my symphonies there and Bär [Beer] played one of my concertos. Presumably the director trumpeted the news about, for Wranizci [Wranitzky], Girowez [Gyrowetz], and our Papa Haydn were present. . . .

Witt's presence in Vienna in 1796 may be the key to the Göttweig parts. The title page, which is reproduced in facsimile, shows clearly that the Monastery acquired the manuscript in 1825: "Synphonia in C/a/2. Violinis. duplo/Flauto Viola/2 Obois/2 Fagottis/2 Corni/2 Clarinis/Tympano, et Basso. dupl./Authore Witt [later 'Witt' underlined in blue pencil]/Comp[aravit] R P Marianus/an. 1825". The reverse sheet of the title page also records two performances at Gött-weig, in connection with the name day of their Patron Saint and founder, Altmanus: "Produit/7 August 1825 ad coenam in [?] fest Altman". and underneath: "29 Aug in fest B. Alt. ad coen:" with no year listed. The watermarks of the parts, however, suggest a date earlier than 1825: three halfmoons, bow and arrow, "AM" (Andrea Mattizzoli, North Italian paper manufacturer), "EGA" under car-touche, sea star with seven arms. These very watermarks are found *in toto* in the original MS. parts to Haydn's *Jahreszeiten* (1802), for instance. The author suggests that the Göttweig source together, with the now lost copy of the D major Symphony, originated in Witt's Viennese visit, and that the Monastery simply acquired them in Vienna more than a quarter of a century later—possibly from one of the Viennese professional copying houses, such as Traeg. That the parts were in any case made *before* 1825 is confirmed by a pencilled date at the end of the first bassoon part: "822" (1822). Originally, more-over, there were more than two symphonies, for "Clarino" It has the following note on the cover:

"6: Sinfonie   di Witt.

No. 1."

This hint led to an examination of other Witt symphonies, in the hopes that perhaps the "Jena" had also been printed under Witt's name. My friend, Jan LaRue, kindly supplied the following information, extracted from the *Union Thematic Catalogue of Eighteenth-Century Symphonies.*

Regensburg (Fürstl. Thurn und Taxis Library) owns MS. parts of six additional symphonies, and André printed another eight. Gerber gives 1805 as the date of the earliest of these, but the André Catalogue of 1804 already lists the first two.

---

next page

The "Jena" Symphony: MS as Friedrich Witt in the Benedictine Monastery of Göttweig in Lower Austria.

Work and key	*Publisher's Number*
I, II, B flat and D major	1886, 1887 (D major in MS. formerly in Göttweig)
III, F major	2354
IV, E flat	2367
V, D major	2622
VI, A minor ("Turque")	2369
VII, C major	3013
VIII, E major	3014

The Zentralbibliothek in Zürich owns two Witt symphonies printed by André, catalogued as AMG XIII, 3011 and 3012. These numbers are not however, André numbers, as one might think from looking at symphonies VII and VIII; they turn out to be local catalogue numbers for copies of André Nos. III and IV. The author is indebted to Director Ernst Hess for clearing up this minor mystery.

At this point, it seemed wise to consult Stein's article in *SIMG*, which the author had not read for several years. Although the "Jena" parts could only be studied *via* Stein, they are so carefully described that the Gordian knot could be untied at once: in short, the "Jena" parts were originally acquired as Witt, and later the title page was lost, subsequent to which someone added Beethoven's name on the two parts. In other words, no "Jena" Symphony by Ludwig van Beethoven really ever existed.

Stein described the watermarks of the "Jena" source, and actually reproduces them in facsimile (letters "JAS", crowned coat-of-arms within which are crossed swords and a series of *fleurs-de-lys*); he adds (p. 135): "I could find paper of this kind only in one other work among the music of the archives: an A major Symphony by Friedrich Witt, all the wind parts of which contain the same watermarks". Secondly, the "Jena" Symphony had an old catalogue number, "24", while the A major Symphony by Witt was "26"; obviously Jena purchased a series of Witt symphonies, including the present work. Thirdly—and with this the puzzle was solved—the first violin part of the "Jena" manuscript had the following initials in the lower right-hand corner (Stein p. 136): "P.F:W:". Stein attempts to connect these with Beethoven's friend and biographer Franz Wegeler ("Possesor . . ."). Of course the initials F. W. stand for none other than Friedrich Witt.

BIBLIOGRAPHY

Allgemeine Musikalische Zeitung (edited by J. F. Rochlitz), Leipzig, Breitkopf & Härtel. See *Registerband*.

André's Publishers Catalogues (Gesellschaft der Musikfreunde, Vienna), 1804 *et seq.*

Gerber, E. L.: *Neues historisch-biographisches Lexikon der Tonkünstler*, Leipzig, 1814, Vierter Theil (S-Z), pp. 593 *f*.

Landon, H. C. R.: "The original versions of Haydn's first 'Salomon' Symphonies" (*Music Review*, XV/1, 1954, pp. 1 *ff*).
The Symphonies of Joseph Haydn, London, 1955, p. 557, n. 8.

Schiedermaier, L.: "Die Blütezeit der Öttingen-Wallerstein'schen Hofkapelle" (*SIMG*, IX, 1907-1908, pp. 83 *ff*).

Simpson, R.: "Observations on the 'Jena' Symphony" (*Music Survey*, II/3, 1950, pp. 155 *ff.*).

Stein, Fritz: "Eine unbekannte Jugendsymphonie Beethoven's?" (*SIMG*, XIII, 1911-1912, pp. 127 *ff.*).

Full and miniature score of the "Jena" Symphony, Leipzig. Breitkopf & Härtel, 1911. Min. score still available.

Arrangement for piano, four hands, by Max Reger.

11. Haydn's "Creation"

On 23, 26, 28 May and 1 June 1791, a great Handel festival was given at Westminster Abbey in London. One thousand performing forces, including double bassoons, "large double Basses", "double bass Kettle drums" (tuned an octave lower than the normal timpani) and a gigantic collection of wind and string instruments performed *Zadok the Priest*, *Israel in Egypt*, *Messiah*, organ concerti, extracts from *Saul*, *Esther*, *Judas Maccabeus*, *Deborah*, *Joseph*, *Joshua*, *Occasional Oratorio*, *Athalia* and *Samson*. Among the audience was Joseph Haydn, then at the summit of his powers and enjoying a spectacularly successful visit to the British capital, where his symphonies were soon to be "received with absolute shouts of applause" (*Morning Chronicle*, April 9, 1794).

Haydn was stunned. Of course he had known a certain amount of Handel, which Gottfried van Swieten (1734-1803), Austrian diplomat and later Chief Librarian of the Austrian National Library, had taken back to Vienna from Berlin and had performed at his concerts in the great hall of the National Library; but such large-scale Handel as he can have heard in Vienna must have been performed without much sense of Handelian tradition, and the works were generally re-orchestrated by Mozart or others to bring them into line with the taste and orchestration of the 1780s. Gone were those stunning high trumpets and the blocked masses of wind instruments, the darting strings of *Why do the Nations* were re-worked into a kind of super Coronation-Mass orchestration.

When Haydn, who had a box near the King in Westminster Abbey, saw His Majesty George III stand up, and with him the entire congregation, for the *Hallelujah Chorus* in *Messiah*, the world's most celebrated composer burst into tears and cried out, "He is the master of us all". To his friend William Shield, the English composer, Haydn said, after hearing *The nations tremble* from *Joshua*, that "he had long been acquainted with music, but never knew half its powers before he heard [Handel]". Haydn's Italian biographer, Giuseppe Carpani, later reported: "Haydn confessed to me that when he heard the music of Hendl [*sic*] in London, he was struck as if he had been put back to the beginning of his studies and had known nothing up to that moment. He meditated on every note and drew from those most learned scores the essence of true musical grandeur."

All during his two visits to England, the idea of choral music on a Handelian scale was at the back of Haydn's fertile mind. In 1792, he tried his hand at what he called a *Madrigal*, in reality a piece for soloists, chorus and orchestra entitled *The Storm*. But it was difficult to organize a chorus, and Haydn's first successful attempt at English words did not yield further efforts. Two years later, in 1794, his friend Lord Abingdon gave him an oratorio entitled *Mare Clausum*, but the composer only finished two numbers, possibly because the text was so dreadful ("For England had great wealth posses'd by sea's access, and thereby blest with plenties not a few, which next the virtue of thy watchful eyes will her secure from foreign miseries . . .").

The Italian oratorio tradition was, in fact, very different from the Handelian type. Haydn had composed one of the former, *Il ritorno di Tobia* (written in 1774 on a text by Boccherini's brother), and it had been a considerable success when first performed in Vienna in 1775. The critic of the *Realzeitung* noted, "The choruses, especially, glowed with a fire previously known only to Handel's . . ."; but fundamentally the Italian oratorio was simply an *opera seria* in disguise and the text a vaguely religious subject suitable for performance at Lent. There were in general not more choruses in an Italian oratorio than in an Italian opera. Nor was Haydn's next oratorio, *The Seven Words* (c. 1786), designed to bring him nearer to the Handelian model; for *The Seven Words* was a highly specialized orchestral work, written on commission for Cadiz Cathedral and consisting of meditations on the Seven Words, preceded by an Overture and concluding with a description of the Earthquake.

It was, nevertheless, *The Seven Words* that turned out to pave the way for *The Creation*. When Haydn was passing through Passau on his way to England in January, 1794, he happened to arrive in time to hear an arrangement of his Oratorio, with a vocal text added (and also some new recitatives), performed in Passau Cathedral. The arrangement was made by the local Cathedral Chapel Master, Joseph Fribert, and Haydn said of it, in his usual laconic way, "I think I could have done the vocal parts better". When he returned to Vienna in the autumn of 1795, Haydn mentioned the Passau affair to Gottfried van Swieten, with whom he had been acquainted since the 1770s; and van Swieten offered to rework the Passau text to suit Haydn's taste. Haydn added the vocal parts (and also some instrumental parts, such as trombones), composed a new interlude for large wind band, and made some other changes; the new version was completed in 1796 and first performed on 26 March of that year at the Schwarzenberg Palace in Vienna. The work was more of a success in this new version (though some Haydn scholars believe the first version to be finer), and the critical approbation seems to have encouraged both composer and author (or rather re-writer). "Haydn", said van Swieten, "we would like to have another oratorio from you!" Suddenly Haydn remembered that he had been carrying round the libretto of an English oratorio which his friend and impresario Johann Peter Salomon had given him in London. Salomon understood Haydn and his music—it will be recalled that the great German violinist had brought him to England and that Haydn had written his twelve famous London, or *Salomon* Symphonies for him—and realized that Haydn had the makings of a great choral composer in him. He had given Haydn the textbook, but Haydn seems to have been worried that his English was not up to such a complicated task.

Haydn, in 1796 and 1797, had been devoting all his energies to choral music: the first two of the last six masses which he wrote every year for the Name Day of Princess Esterházy. Both works, the *Missa Sancti Bernardi de Offida* (known as the *Heiligmesse*) and the *Missa in tempore belli* (known as the *Paukenmesse*), show that Haydn had absorbed, and re-created in his own language, the great Handelian tradition. He was ready for the big task, spiritually and musically.

The first dated reference to Haydn's *Creation* occurs, curiously, in a letter from the famous theoretician and contrapuntalist J. G. Albrechtsberger to his and Haydn's erstwhile pupil, Ludwig van Beethoven. On 15 December 1796 Albrechtsberger writes: "Haydn came to see me yesterday; he is occupied with the idea of a big oratorio which he intends to call *The Creation*, and he hopes to finish the work soon. He improvised some of it for me and I think it will be very good."

Van Swieten, although a man of letters and politics, was also a composer, whose symphonies, Haydn once said rather grimly, "were as stiff as the Baron himself". He thus understood the problems of a composer *vis-à-vis* the libretto and he did everything to make it easier for

Haydn. He later (1799) describes his part in the venture in an article written for the *Allgemeine Musikalische Zeitung:*

"My part in the work, which was originally of English origin, is perhaps rather more than that of a mere translator; but not by any means so extensive that I could call the text my own. It was written by an unknown person [Griesinger, Haydn's first biographer, calls him a Mr. Lidley or Lindley], who put it together largely from Milton's *Paradise Lost,* and intended it for Handel. It is not known why this great composer never made any use of the work; but when Haydn was in London, the text was brought forth and it was suggested that he set it to music. At first glance Haydn found the material of the text well chosen, but he did not accept the offer immediately and said he would give his answer when he returned to Vienna. He then showed it to me here, and I agreed with his judgment of the piece. Moreover, I saw immediately that this work would provide Haydn with an ideal opportunity to display the full powers of his inexhaustible genius; and as I had long hoped for this very possibility, I was encouraged to take the libretto and to give the English poem a German setting. In this way the present translation came into being; and while on the whole I followed the general outlines of the original piece, I changed details whenever it seemed prudent to do so for the sake of the musical line or expression".

By a stroke of good fortune, van Swieten's autograph of the libretto, which Haydn of course owned, has come down to us; after Haydn's death in 1809, Prince Esterházy purchased Haydn's legacy, which included a huge collection of opera and oratorio libretti, apart from music; and this collection has for the most part survived World War II's fighting in Budapest and is now in that city's National Library. In the margins, the Baron wrote useful and highly intelligent suggestions, most of which Haydn accepted gladly. To illustrate, here is the beginning of the Oratorio, with Swieten's comments (we have left the German text of the work itself untranslated) (next page):

Die Schöpfung ein Oratorium
Erster Teil
Erster Auftritt
Ouverture: die Vorstellung
des Chaos
Ein Engel: Recitativ mit
Begleitung. Basso
Im Anfange schuf Gott
Himmel und Erde;
und die Erde war ohne Form
und leer; und Finsterniß war
auf der Fläche.
Chor
Und der Geist Gottes schwebte
auf der Fläche der Wasser;
und Gott sprach: Es werde
Licht, und es ward Licht.

Recitative. Tenore
Und Gott sah das Licht,
dass es gut war; und Gott
schied das Licht von der
Finsterniß.
Aria. Tenore
Nun schwanden vor dem
     heiligen Strahle
Des schwarzen Dunkels
     gräuliche Schatten.
Der erste Tag entstand.
Verwirrung weicht, und
     Ordnung keimt empor.
Erstarrt, entflieht der
     Höllengeister Schaar.
In des Abgrunds Tiefen hinab,
Zur ewigen Nacht
Chor
Verzweiflung, Wuth und
     Schrecken
Begleiten ihren Sturz,
Und eine neue Welt
Entspringt auf Gotteswort.

Personen
Mehrere Engel.
Adam.
Eva.

The descriptive passages of the Overture could serve as accompaniment to this Recitative.

In this chorus the Darkness could disappear gradually, but in such a way that enough of the Darkness remain to make the sudden transition to light very effective.
"Es werde Licht etc."
["And there was light"]
must only be said once.

It would be a good thing if the final ritornello of the aria were to announce the chorus, and if the chorus were to begin at once, so as to express the emotions of the fleeing Spirits of Hell.

Next to No. 28 of Part III (*Von Deiner Güt, o Herr und Gott*), which is entitled *Song of Praise with alternating choruses of Angels*, Swieten wrote *inter alia* "Since at this point the first, still inexperienced and innocent pair of human beings expresses their innermost feelings, it is a matter of course that the song be simple and the melody proceed syllabically; but Adam could have a stronger gait to his that Eva to hers, and the difference in their emotions that their diverse sex entails could perhaps be suggested by alternating major and minor keys."

As can be seen, Haydn followed this suggestion, too (but of course he followed the spirit rather than the letter, as will be observed). Thus the Baron's participation in the success of the Oratorio is considerably greater than that of the average eighteenth-century librettist, and quite different from, say, da Ponte's contribution to Mozart's libretti. The text of *The Creation* was not liked in some quarters, especially in northern Germany; and it is quite true that while Vienna was the centre of the world, musically, and was to remain so for another thirty years, its people were always less interested in literature as such, and less well educated: it was not entirely their fault, for Schiller's dramas were considered too "hot" politically and were banned by the Austrian censor, and it will be recalled that *Le mariage de Figaro* as a play was banned and could only insinuate itself across the boards via da Ponte and Mozart. Nevertheless, modern scholarship has begun to reinstate van Swieten. Martin Stern, in a recently published and brilliant article on *Spirit and Origin of the van Swieten Libretto* (*Haydn Studien*, Cologne 1966, Vol. 1, Heft 3), writes:

"*The Creation* brought in the biggest box-office returns in the history of Vienna; it conquered, in one fell swoop, about the turn of the century, a Europe divided by war; it reunited all classes—Catholic Austria, Anglican England, Evangelical Berlin and even a laicized Paris—in admiration, and repeatedly moved thousands and thousands of listeners to tears of devotion and emotion. It brought, with the approval of the First Consul, to the composer the highest musical order that the French Republic could confer, and remained the most frequently performed choral composition in Prussia for decades. To all this van Swieten's text contributed its part, though that part is difficult to measure precisely. If one reads the letters of gratitude and the reports of those performances which were sent to Haydn, or circulated and/or published by listeners and critics, one begins to get the impression that in this libretto the wishes and dreams of a whole generation were realized artistically; for otherwise such an echo cannot be explained. To have realized

M

these needs shows that van Swieten, even if not primarily creative, must have had astounding powers of perception amounting almost to seismographic sensitivity. . . . For not only Haydn, since the deaths of Gluck and Mozart unquestionably the leading composer of his age, but also van Swieten might have said that his language was understood by the whole world.''

In its fundamental appeal to the Brotherhood of Man, Haydn's *Creation* is close to the Masonic message of Mozart's *Magic Flute*, a fact which did not escape audiences then. Freemasonry had been banned by the new and conservative Emperor Franz on 2 January 1795 (and was never again allowed officially in Austria until the Monarchy was dissolved in 1918) but as in the case of Mozart's *Figaro*, "what cannot be said may be sung"; and all the King's censors and all the King's men could not prevent Haydn from writing music—in the words of the old Masonic charter—to "unite in true friendship men who otherwise would have remained strangers". We do not know if van Swieten had been a Freemason; but Haydn, like Mozart, had been one. There is little doubt that some of this basic Masonic message in the *Creation*—what Martin Stern (*vide supra*) calls "Verkündigung gott-ebenbildlicher Humanität" (which we may rather freely translate as the "propagation of a humanity in God's image")—is derivative of the period of enlightenment which, in Austria, had blossomed into flower under the liberal and tolerant views of Emperor Joseph II (died 1790). *The Creation* is perhaps the last witness, and one of the most moving, of a great humanitarian era in Central Europe, a truly golden age which was soon to disappear for ever.

Naturally, the production of a huge work which required an enormous orchestra, a large chorus, and soloists needed a special kind of financial backing. Van Swieten had formed a musical society, of which he was secretary, to help finance his Handel and Bach productions; this *Gesellschaft der Associirten*, as it was called, included the flower of the Austro-Hungarian nobility; its roll-call was rather like reading the *Almanach de Gotha*—Liechtenstein, Esterházy, Schwarzenberg, Lobkowitz, Auersperg, Kinsky, Lichnowsky, Trautmannsdorf, Zinzerndorf, Czernin, Harrach, Erdödy, Apponyi, Fries. . . . These gentlemen guaranteed Haydn the sum of 500 ducats and agreed to underwrite all the costs. Prince Schwarzenberg offered his magnificent winter palace on the New Market Place (am neuen Markt), and Haydn assembled the best Viennese instrumentalists and singers for the occasion. The three principal soloists were Christine Gerardi, Mathias Rathmayer and Ignaz Saal; the famous composer Salieri sat at the piano-

forte. The general rehearsal was on 29 April 1798 and the first performance the next day. Such was the excitement of the city that eighteen
mounted and twelve foot police were engaged to control the crowds,
and this despite the semi-private nature of the performance. *The
Creation* was an enormous success, the greatest Haydn had enjoyed
since London. The Society promptly arranged two further performances, on 7 and 10 May, at the second of which, noted Count Zinzerndorf in his diary, "on distribuoit des vers imprimés a son [Haydn's]
honneur".

Haydn very often made changes, generally in the instrumental and
dynamic details, after the first performance of a new work. *The Creation*
was no exception. He had worked very hard on the Oratorio, and some
of his fascinating and detailed sketches have been preserved. "I was
never so religious as during the composition of *The Creation*", he told
his biographer Griesinger. "Daily I fell on my knees and asked God
for strength." Now, after the initial excitement was over, Haydn made
a number of small but important improvements. The trombones were
added when the whole orchestra bursts into the C major majesty of
And there was Light; pizzicato strings were put in to sustain the three
solo flutes at the beginning of Part III; *Be fruitful,* originally a *secco*
recitative, gained its present, and wonderfully effective, orchestration
of lower (divided) strings. The author of these notes discovered the
entire original performance material of *The Creation* in the Vienna
Rathaus some years ago, which enables us to see these changes; the
autograph has long disappeared.

Next season, Haydn wanted another semi-private performance of
his work before offering it to the public; and the *Gesellschaft der
Associirten*, at the Schwarzenberg Palais, sponsored two performances,
on 2 and 4 March 1799. Speaking of the Trio just before the final
chorus of Part II, *Den Atem hauchst du wieder aus und neues Leben
sprosst hervor*, Count Zinzerndorf wrote, on 4 March, in his Diary:
"Ces mots surtout si bien accompagnés pénètrent l'âme d'une sainte
veneration". The public concert, planned for 19 March 1799, was
arranged by Swieten's Society; they paid the expenses and turned
over the entire box-office receipts to Haydn. The excitement was tremendous; all the boxes of the Burgtheater (where Mozart's *Figaro* had
been launched not quite thirteen years earlier) were sold out by the
middle of February. A friend of Haydn's, Joseph Carl Rosenbaum
(whose wife, Therese née Gassmann sang many of the soprano parts

in Haydn's masses), describes getting into the theatre:

"Tuesday, 19th. . . . At about 4 o'clock Agnes and Tonerl and I went to Haydn's concert at the Burg Theater. Never since the theatre was built has there been such a fearful and dangerous press of people. Pfersman let us through the office and gallery to the box-office, and we were thus able to get good seats.—Casanova [brother of the famous author] was also there and, as it happened, sat next to me; we conversed together. Before *The Creation* began there were . . . incidents [because of the crowds battling to get seats] . . .".

The critic of the *Allgemeine Musikalische Zeitung* in Leipzig wrote:

"On the 19th inst. I heard Haydn's *Creation*. Not to report immediately on this happy occasion (for I feel it was such) would show too little feeling for the Art, and for Friendship. The audience was exceptionally large and the receipts amounted to 4,088 fl. 3 kr.—a sum which had never been taken by any Viennese theatre. Apart from this, the aristocracy guaranteed the by no means inconsiderable costs. One can hardly imagine the silence and the attention with which the work was received, broken only by soft exclamations at the most remarkable passages; at the end of each piece and each section there was enthusiastic applause."

Haydn's biographer, Griesinger, was also present· "I had the good fortune", he relates, "to be a witness to the profound emotion and wild enthusiasm with which this oratorio was greeted by the whole audience when it was played under Haydn's direction. Haydn admitted to me, too, that he could not express the feelings which filled his soul when the performance expressed his every wish, and when the audience awaited every note in profound silence. 'Sometimes my whole body was ice cold', he said. 'and sometimes I was overcome with burning fever; more than once I was afraid that I should suddenly suffer a stroke'."

The soloists were the same except for the soprano Gerardi, who had since married; her place was taken by the daughter of the bass singer, Therese Saal, who rocketed to fame with this performance and, indeed, became inseparably connected to the Oratorio. Salieri sat, as before, at the pianoforte. There is also a report on Haydn's conducting *The Creation* which has come down to us, and although it was written later in the year (for a performance in December), it is appropriate to mention it here.

"I found his mimics [wrote the correspondent of the *Allgemeine Musikalische Zeitung*] most interesting. He was able to breathe upon the numerous performers the spirit in which his work had been composed, and ought to be played. One could read in all his gestures, which were nothing if not exaggerated, very clearly what he thought about each passage and how he must have felt . . .". This shows, incidentally, that Haydn was practising the art of conducting, as we know it, long before Weber, Spohr or any of the other nineteenth-century candidates who have been proposed as the inventors of that art.

Haydn now decided to print the work himself by subscription, instead of giving it to his "sleepy" (Haydn's description) Viennese publishers Artaria. And now comes an extraordinary fact: van Swieten had obviously salvaged as much as he could of the original English textbook, and the score was to be engraved *in two languages*. Haydn knew that he had many friends in England, and he hoped that they would come forward; he was not disappointed. He kept a little hand-written book of the subscribers, and the list was also printed at the beginning of the score. Here is the subscription announcement, which Haydn sent to the *Allgemeine Musikalische Zeitung*:

"The success which my Oratorio, *The Creation* has been fortunate enough to enjoy here, and the wish expressed in the 16th number of the [*Allgemeine*] *Musikalische Zeitung* that its dissemination would not, as was often the case previously, be left to those abroad, have moved me to arrange for its distribution myself.

Thus the work is to appear in three or four months, neatly and correctly engraved and printed on good paper, with German and English texts; and in full score, so that, on the one hand, the public may have the work in its entirety, and so that the connoisseur may see it *in toto* and thus better judge it; while on the other, it will be easier to prepare the parts, should one wish to perform the work anywhere.

The price of the Oratorio, which will consist of some 300 pages, is to be 3 ducats, or 13 Fl. 30 Kr. in Viennese currency; and although payment does not need to be made until delivery, I wish nevertheless that those who contemplate its purchase would inform me provisionally thereof, and give me their names, in order that they may appear in the subscription list at the front of the score.

The actual appearance of the Oratorio in print—every copy will be signed—will be announced by a special notice, when the time comes.

Vienna, 15th June 1799
> Joseph Haydn,
> Doctor of Music, *Kapellmeister* in the Service of His Highness the Prince Esterhàzy, and Member of the Royal Swedish Musical Academy.

In Vienna, Vorstadt Gumpendorf, untere Steingasse, Nr. 73."

He sent this announcement with an interesting letter to the publishers of the paper, Messrs. Breitkopf & Härtel of Leipzig:

"Vienna, 12th June 1799.

Dearest Friend!

I am really very much ashamed to have to offend a man who has written so often and honoured me with so many marks of esteem (which I do not deserve), by answering him at this late date; it is not negligence on my part but the vast amount of BUSINESS which is responsible, and the older I get, the more business I have to transact daily. I only regret that on account of my growing age and (unfortunately) the decrease of my mental powers, I am able to dispatch but the smallest part of it. Every day the world pays me compliments on the fire of my recent works, but no one will believe the strain and effort it costs me to produce them: there are some days in which my enfeebled memory and the unstrung state of my nerves crush me to the earth to such an extent that I fall prey to the worst sort of depression, and thus am quite incapable of finding even a single idea for many days thereafter; until at last Providence revives me, and I can again sit down at the pianoforte and begin to scratch away again. Enough of this! . . .

I WOULD ONLY WISH, AND HOPE, THAT THE CRITICS DO NOT DEAL TOO SEVERELY WITH MY CREATION: THEY MIGHT PERHAPS OBJECT A LITTLE TO THE MUSICAL ORTHOGRAPHY OF CERTAIN PASSAGES, AND POSSIBLY SOME OTHER MINOR POINTS ELSEWHERE; BUT THE TRUE CONNOISSEUR WILL SEE THE REASONS FOR THEM AS READILY AS I DO, AND WILL PUSH ASIDE THIS STUMBLING-BLOCK. NULLA REGOLA S[ENZA] E [CCEZIONE]."

The next year *The Creation* made its triumphal way to Paris, to London, to Berlin and Prague. Until he was no longer able to do so, Haydn conducted a yearly Viennese performance of the work, usually for some charitable organization; his last public appearance was for a performance in 1808, which Salieri directed, and to which all the great artists of Vienna (including Gyrowetz, Beethoven, and Hummel) came to pay their last homage. At the passage *And there was light*, Haydn was quite overcome, and said: "It was not I, but a Power above who created that." But the strain proved too much for the old man, and he had to be carried out after the first part. Beethoven bent down and kissed his hand and forehead, and most of the audience was in tears. As he reached the door, Haydn told his bearers to turn him to the orchestra, and after lifting his hand, as if in the act of benediction, he was carried out into the night.

The construction of *The Creation* is, musically speaking, traditional; that is, Haydn uses the customary division of choruses, accompanied recitatives (usually for descriptive passages), arias, and *secco* recitatives (with harpsichord and lower strings only). It seems quite clear that he retained the old-fashioned Italian *secco* for reasons of colour; in these brief sections, the listener has a chance to rest from the vast sound of the choruses and the largest orchestra Haydn ever employed. In the choruses, solo voices are also used. This is a direct result, not only of the older oratorio form, but of Haydn's late Masses, in which one of the most important structural features is the constant juxtaposition of choir and soloists. The orchestra itself consists of three flutes, two oboes, two clarinets, two bassoons, contra-bassoon, two horns, two trumpets, three trombones, kettledrums, and strings; and never is Haydn more brilliant and resourceful than in the instrumentation of *The Creation*. The "boundless loneliness" of the introduction, a *Description of Chaos*, is positively breath-taking, not only in its harmonic modernity (*e.g.* the *Tristan*-like augmented chords at the end) but also in its marvellous orchestration (the wild sweep of the clarinet, and the almost sinister, grey woodwind scoring which so movingly depicts the earth surrounded by swirling darkness). And when has Haydn—or, indeed, any other composer—surpassed the serene, unearthly beauty of the E major introduction to Part III, describing that magical moment of early morning when the sun first touches "the rosy clouds"? (It is here that the three flutes are used.)

There are, of course, sublime high-points: the unforgettable exaltation of *And there was light*, a tremendous, overwhelming fortissimo; the shining D major brightness of the first rising sun, and the soft sheen of the strings as Uriel describes in hushed tones the first moonlight; *The heavens are telling*, the chorus, based on Psalm XIX 1, that ends the first part, in which we feel that truly Haydn was there "when the morning stars sang together, and all the sons of God shouted for joy"; Raphael's awesome description of the impenetrable mystery of birth, in which divided violas, cellos, and the bottom range of the double-basses (a brilliant afterthought—originally this was a recitative *secco*) underline God's command: *Be fruitful, grow and multiply!* But there are many similar inspirations throughout the work.

The descriptions of nature, of birds and beasts, are not without their moments of humour. How the audience must have been delighted with the roars of the "tawny lion" (with *fortissimo* double-bassoon and trombones), the snarls of the tiger, and the loathsome course of crawling worm (No. 21). Some of the arias are so far removed from the *da capo* Italian form that they might more profitably be compared to the early romantic *Lied:* such an aria is Uriel's *In native worth*, the joyous affirmation of the brotherhood of man. If the text perhaps reminds us of Mozart's *Magic Flute*, the modulations (such as that of bars 48*ff*, from the dominant of F major to D flat and A flat) look far forward to the enchanted harmonic world of Schubert. But only Haydn could have written the lovely soprano aria *With verdure clad*, a gentle, happy song to the early spring.

Perhaps only an old and very wise man could have written *The Creation;* and perhaps, too, only a sexagenarian could so poignantly recapture the bliss of the early morning, the magic of the moonlight, or the rapture of a spring day: these things which he knows will soon retreat beyond his grasp. That which Carpani, one of three contemporaries who collected material for a biography of Haydn, wrote on hearing a Haydn Mass one Sunday morning might well have been said of *The Creation*: "In 1799", he writes, "I was confined at Vienna by a fever. The bells announced a Mass at a church not far from my room: my *ennui* got the better of my prudence, and I rose and went to console myself with a little music. I inquired as I entered, and found it was the festival of St. Ann, and that they were going to perform a Mass of Haydn's in B flat major,[1] which I had never before heard. Scarcely had it begun before I felt myself affected. I broke out into a perspiration, my headache went away: I left the church with a cheerfulness to which I had long been a stranger, and the fever never returned."

(Autumn 1967)

---

1).   Probably the *Missa Sti. Bernardi de Offida* ("*Heiligmesse*", 1796).

12. The Dawn of the Romantic Period

There are very few periods in musical history whose beginnings and ends can be determined precisely; and there has been much controversy when the Romantic Period began and even if there is such a thing at all. This may be true in retrospect, and it may not materially help us to understand the music of the nineteenth century by calling it Romantic; for it is obvious that such a long period of time would include many schools, many composers, and many different modes of expression. In determining when the Romantic Period began, we have some very valuable evidence which shows that even if we have our doubts about what the word "romantic" means or meant, educated people in the year 1810 had very definite opinions on this subject.

A characteristic figure of the period E. T. A. Hoffman, lawyer, poet, artist (he drew well), composer, music critic, reviewed Beethoven's Fifth Symphony in the *Allgemeine Musikalische Zeitung* of July 1810, by which time the symphony was a couple of years old:

"The reviewer has in front of him one of the most important works of the master [Beethoven], to whom no one these days will deny the first place as a composer of instrumental music; he [the reviewer] is filled with the circumstances about which he is supposed to speak, and nobody should object if he exceeds the boundaries of normal criticism in attempting to put into words everything which he feels so deeply about this composition.

"When music is described as an independent art, we should always mean instrumental music; for it spurns the help of, and interference from, any other art and speaks its own language, pure and characteristic. It is the most romantic of all the arts—one is almost inclined to say: the only *purely* romantic. . . . Haydn and Mozart, the creators of the new instrumental music, first revealed to us the art in its full glory; he who regarded them with complete love and penetrated to their innermost minds is—Beethoven. . . . Beethoven's instrumental music opens to us the world of the monstrous and indefinable. Glowing rays shoot through the deep night of this world and we become aware of huge shadows that weave back and forth, encircling us ever more tightly and destroying everything, leaving only the pain of never-ending longing. . . . Beethoven is a wholly romantic and for that reason a wholly *musical* composer; and that is perhaps why in vocal music, which does not allow for vague longings and only portrays the emotions conjured up by the words . . ., he is less successful; and why also his instrumental music seldom attracts the masses. . . . Deep in Beethoven's soul is the romanticism of music, which he expresses in his works with great genius and contemplation. This reviewer has never felt this more strongly than in the present Symphony where, more than in any other of his works, this romanticism unfolds in one increasing climax to the very end, sweeping the listener inexorably into the fabulous ghost world of the never-ending . . . .

"The reviewer believes he may sum up his opinion of this great work of art by the master in a few words if he says: It is a work of genius, worked out with deep attention and displaying to a very great extent the romanticism of music. . . ''.

Romanticism as a concept is something which could only have happened North of the Alps; the very word comes from eighteenth-century German literature (the German word *Roman*[1] means novel, and *roman-haft* means "like a novel"). In 1802 Schiller called his play *Die Jung-frau von Orleans* a "romantic tragedy". The word romantic soon came to include a large number of concepts, such as: courtly, old-fashioned, naive, redolent of folklore. The romantic world also came to mean a nether-nether fairy-tale atmosphere of magic and supernatural; and it was not long before all this led to the demonic, the sinister, and the world of the deep, green German forest—where it is not hard to imagine that pixies, elves and magicians live.

Haydn had died in 1809 and his death very nearly coincides with Beethoven's Fifth Symphony, which, as we have seen, contemporaries considered a thoroughly romantic composition. Even the rather superficial story which Beethoven is supposed to have told someone, to the effect that the first four notes of the opening movement were like fate knocking on the door, is a thoroughly romantic concept. It is something

1). Closely allied, of course, to the French novel "Romance".

that never would have occurred to Bach or Gluck or Mozart. Things were changing very rapidly in 1810 in a Europe which had been in the throes of the Napoleonic Wars for several years and which would know no peace until 1815 and the Congress of Vienna. Society was no longer divided into such rigid classes as before, and the rising bourgeoisie all over Europe soon came to have as much importance as the aristocracy, which conversely gradually began to lose its age-old importance. People were much more educated. The average musician of 1810 was a much more educated man than his predecessor of thirty years before. Mendelssohn not only composed delightful music but also painted well and wrote brilliantly. E. T. A. Hoffman, whom we have mentioned briefly above, was a typical man of the romantic era—highly educated, from the middle classes, capable of earning a living by his wits and not necessarily by royal or aristocratic patronage, Hoffman exacted a considerable influence in Germany on the intellectual life of his contemporaries.

Mozart, from the evidence of his letters, hardly seems to have been interested in nature at all. One of the typical manifestations of the romantic man was his interest in, indeed his compulsive fascination about, the outdoor world. We have a sheet of paper in Beethoven's hand which reads as follows: "In the country it is as if every tree spoke to me—holy! holy! In the forests what delight! Who can describe it?"

Beethoven's biographer Anton Felix Schindler had this to say about Beethoven:

"It would be a grave error to suppose that Beethoven's love of the out-of-doors was merely the result of a predilection for beautiful scenery or of a need for physical exercise. . . . The present author, who had the great pleasure of accompanying Beethoven on countless walks through the open country over hills and dales, is moreover in the position to state that the master was frequently his nature guide and this instruction was generally more enthusiastic and lengthy than his music teaching. Let us put it more clearly by saying that in Beethoven we have a man in whom nature was fully personified."[2]

Of course, the "Pastoral Symphony" was one tangible result of this involvement with nature. The green German forest is also a central

---

2). From *Beethoven as I Knew Him*, a biography of Anton Felix Schindler, edited by Donald W. MacArdle, translated by S. Jolly, Faber, London 1966, pp. 143 *f.*

part of Carl Maria von Weber's *Der Freischütz*, first produced at Berlin on 18 June 1821. Here we have the prototype of German romantic music. It is interesting to note that *Freischütz* has always been one of the most popular operas in German speaking countries but has never attracted the Italians; and indeed the then celebrated Italian operatic composer Spontini, a rival of Weber's in Berlin, called *Freischütz* a "piece of romantic childishness".

Scholars have never been in agreement as to whether Beethoven was a classicist or a romanticist; I would say that he was both, and that both elements are strongly prominent in his music. But Franz Schubert, who died only two years after Beethoven, was a much more typically romantic composer. It seems, after the death of Beethoven, to have been increasingly difficult for composers to write symphonies. One thinks of Brahms' fearful comment, recalling how the presence of Beethoven hung heavy over the nineteenth century: "I feel the giant footsteps behind me". Thus it is not surprising to see that shorter forms soon flourished in the Romantic Period, intimate music for home consumption. Here we find the impromptu, ballade, the *moment musical*, and Mendelssohn's *Lieder ohne Worte* (songs without words). In the orchestra the woodwind came to occupy an increasingly prominent role, partly because of the technical improvements made on the instruments: Böhm revolutionized the construction of the flute, and to the French horn, and soon afterwards to the trumpet, were added valves by which those instruments could for the first time in their history play all the chromatic notes of the scale. One of the first pieces of music to use such a valved horn is the famous fourth horn solo in the slow movement of Beethoven's Ninth Symphony. Romantic composers had a natural predilection for clarinets and horns, and again the horn was closely allied to the hunt and thus to the dark green woods and the fairy-tale world of *Freischütz*.

It was, however, the piano which now became the household instrument and the principal vehicle for most composers (a violin virtuoso like Paganini, of course, excepted). There were two principal schools of piano manufacturers and piano composers—London and Vienna; and since there was much interchange between the two, it may be said that they fructified each other. Beethoven began his career as a piano virtuoso, so did Schubert and so after him did Chopin and Liszt. While it was unthinkable that a composer of 1730 could have not been proficient on several instruments and certainly know the technique of the violin, by 1830 it was possible for Chopin to have composed and performed a piano concerto without really knowing the technique of orchestration. Indeed, almost the whole of Chopin's output is devoted to the piano, something which hardly had ever happened before even in the case of such a famous harpsichord virtuoso as Domenico Scarlatti, who of course composed all sorts of other kinds of music including operas.

Composers soon began to have extra-musical thoughts and reactions. They also began to write down some of their aesthetic beliefs. We need only recall such a frantic outburst as the Beethoven *Heiligenstädter Testament* to realize that it would hardly have occurred to an eighteenth-century composer to put down *in writing* such personal thoughts. There also began, even at this early period, that fatal division between the artist and his public, between the dream world of the composer and the down-to-earth world of concert life. The style of music began to change with a fantastic rapidity. Consider that in 1830—three years after Beethoven's death—we have the Chopin E minor piano concerto (Op. 11), Schumann's Op. 1 and Berlioz' *Symphonie Fantastique*. The "new romantics", as they are now called, began to sweep Europe. In 1843, Wagner composed the *Flying Dutchman* and two years after that *Tannhäuser*.

As early as *c.* 1815 there began to be a violent division between North and South. We have mentioned that the romantic movement was a typical manifestation of Northern Europe, and so it was that Rossini and the new Italian school soon became a kind of *anti*-romantic movement. When Rossini came to Vienna between 1815 and 1820 Italian opera soon became the popular rage; the German group put up *Freischütz* and later *Euryanthe*, another successful opera by Weber, against the Italian group, but they misunderstood the crisis: Rossini in his operas appeared to many intelligent Viennese to incorporate the essence of sanity, beauty, and uncomplicated, glorious music. This new Italian school, which at this early period was based on the classical forms and orchestration of Haydn and Mozart, soon developed into Bellini, Donizetti, and the hard realism of the young Verdi. This *anti*-romantic movement continued in Italy to exist throughout the nineteenth century. This was also the last golden age of *belcanto*[3], and even

---

3). *Belcanto* continued, of course, into the twentieth century; but its death more or less coincided with the death of one of its greatest exponents, Enrico Caruso (1873-1921).

Beethoven admired the Italian school and technique of singing.

One of the curious side-lines of the romantic movement was its interest in the past. Musicians now became interested in Palestrina and Bach. In 1829 Mendelssohn conducted the first modern performance of Bach's *Matthew Passion* in Berlin and thus restored to permanent concert life one of the great monuments of Western man.

This was also the age in which the waltz as an art form came to occupy an increasingly prominent position. J. Lanner and the Strauß dynasty composed waltzes for orchestra of an artistic level such as Haydn, Mozart and Beethoven had expended on their own German Dances and minuets for dancing. The operetta came to be an art form of its own and reached a climax in the works of Offenbach and such a piece as Johann Strauß' *Fledermaus*.

Various mechanical improvements were of great assistance to the composers, and not only as regards the wind instruments mentioned above. The piano soon became the modern instrument we know today, and Liszt's mature music was composed for an instrument which hardly sounds any different than our modern Steinway and Bechstein. A Viennese colleague of Beethoven called Mälzel invented the metronome which allowed composers for the first time to show the precise tempo in which they wanted their pieces to be performed. The new and mechanically improved wind instruments soon allowed composers to write in distant keys and to make modulations which were either impossible or extremely difficult to execute in the late eighteenth century. One remembers that contemporary German newspapers often complained about the difficulty of the wind parts in Mozart's operas. The famous "*Tristan*-chord" at the beginning of Wagner's opera of that name, and indeed the whole chromatic widening of Wagner and later Debussy, would not have been possible without these technical improvements.

But whereas the eighteenth century was basically one musical world, so that Haydn when he went to England in 1791, upon being reminded that he spoke no English could truthfully answer: "My language is understood all over the world"; the musical world of the nineteenth century, agitated by political and social upheavals of an unprecedented strength, began gradually to split up into national and regional schools whose products were not necessarily understood when they were exported across their home borders. It all too soon became commonplace for composers to be misunderstood or hardly appreciated away from their own countries. Even today controversy still rages about the music of Bruckner, Delius and Sibelius. The tragedy of that modern gap between composer and public had begun and as the nineteenth century progressed, and the fresh and delightful impetus of the early romantic movement grew faded, other, grimmer problems began to beset the world and the composers who lived in it.

January 1968

General Index

Index Of Works